P9-DFM-563

Date Due

BANKING ON THE WORLD

BANKING ON THE WORLD ❊ ❊

THE POLITICS OF
AMERICAN INTERNATIONAL
FINANCE

JEFFRY A. FRIEDEN

HARPER & ROW, PUBLISHERS *New York*
Cambridge, Philadelphia, San Francisco, Washington
1817 *London, Mexico City, São Paulo, Singapore, Sydney*

FIRST EDITION

Designer: Sidney Feinberg

Copy editor: Carole Berglie

Indexer: Auralie Logan

Library of Congress Cataloging-in-Publication Data

Frieden, Jeffry A.
Banking on the world.

Bibliography: p.
Includes index.
1. International finance. 2. Banks and banking,
International. 3. Banks and banking, American.
I. Title.
HG3881.F735 1988   332.1'5'0973   87-45136
ISBN 0-06-015822-0

87 88 89 90 91 HC 10 9 8 7 6 5 4 3 2 1

Contents

Acknowledgments

Hundreds of bankers, government officials, journalists, scholars, and others were kind enough to grant me interviews and other information, and I am grateful to them. I am especially indebted to the many other friends and colleagues who assisted in various ways with the writing of *Banking on the World*: Aaron Asher, Sarah Bartlett, Bill Brand, Lawrence Broz, Scott Bruckner, David Dollar, Graham Ingham, David Lake, Katie Martin, William McNeil, John Michel, Nora Monk, Ken Sokoloff, Joan Spero, Susan Strange, and Andrew Wylie. As always, the members of my family were my severest critics and strongest supporters.

A note on references: where no citation is given, a quotation's source was a personal interview.

1

The United States in the World Economy

International finance is the pivot around which the world economy twists and turns, and it affects politics and economics in every nation. Money and capital markets around the world are part of a global financial system in which all firms and investors compete continually with their counterparts in other countries. Every day hundreds of billions of dollars in stocks, bonds, and currencies speed electronically from trading room to trading room in search of a higher rate of return, so that Singapore and Paris, or London and Panama, are financially as close as midtown Manhattan and Wall Street. These enormous capital flows have blurred the lines between national financial markets, and have changed the environment within which investors, managers, workers, and politicians operate.

The United States is not immune to the rigors of this global financial integration. Rumors on overseas currency markets can drive the dollar up or down in an hour, make it difficult for the U.S. government to sell its bonds, or suck tens of billions of dollars out of or into Wall Street. International financial markets had enough faith in the Reagan administration's economic policies in the early 1980s that they were willing to finance enormous budget deficits. Yet as the ensuing flood of foreign capital rushed toward the United States, it drove the dollar's international value up by half, priced most American goods out of world markets, and filled American stores with cheap imports. As the rust bowl and farm belts reeled, hundreds of pieces of protectionist legislation were introduced in Congress, while the nation's booming financial, commercial, service, and military sectors thrived on the influx of foreign finance and goods.

If the United States, with the world's largest economy, is whipsawed by international financial trends, the economic and political fortunes of smaller nations can be overturned in a matter of weeks. Even as capital scurried to the United States in 1982, the world's bankers lost faith in borrowers in the Third World. Economies all over Africa, Asia, and Latin America collapsed, and governments from Manila to Brasília followed suit shortly thereafter. American bank depositors discovered uneasily that their savings had been lent to countries they had never heard of, and financial systems around the world staggered.

Global financial markets are the centerpiece of the contemporary world economic order, which was built largely by the United States in the aftermath of World War II. America's international bankers, indeed, led the charge toward today's global economic integration. In the 1950s, after twenty-five years of depression, war, and reconstruction, a few large banks from New York, Boston, Chicago, and San Francisco began to expand their foreign operations. The cautious early moves toward international financial openness were not controversial; the growing global banking system was barely noticed, for the United States was fully able to lead and manage world economic interaction, while general postwar prosperity minimized the need for such management. As economic growth slowed and the international economy became more and more intertwined, especially in the financial realm, the preexisting consensus eroded. All governments, including that of the United States, found it increasingly difficult to control international economic transactions and to shield domestic groups from the often undesirable effects of international flows of goods and capital.

Since the early 1970s, international banking has been the world economy's leading growth area. Today's $3 trillion global financial market has become a force that no one bank, group of banks, or government can control, nor can it easily be stuffed back behind national borders. The world economy is riding a huge and very demanding tiger whose ferocity is untested.

The effects of global banking are both economic and political, and they are felt both in relations between nations and inside the nations themselves. Financial markets are the nerve center of modern capitalist economies; they channel investment capital toward new profit opportunities, and move capital away from troubled firms and industries. The more rapidly and effectively financial markets operate, the more exacting is the discipline they impose on shareholders, corporate managers, and employees. In addition to their importance to domestic economic and political trends, financial flows across national borders are inherently the stuff of which world politics is made. International and domestic politics and economics are inextricably interrelated in any discussion of banking today.

We must untangle these intermingled causes and effects to explain how the world's financial system got where it is and to predict where it might go. Our analytical point of departure is that economic actors in society—firms, investors, economic interest groups—have political preferences that reflect their material interests. Firms that depend on government contracts lobby for these contracts; banks with overseas assets insist that the government help protect these assets; industries in difficulty press for government subsidies or tariff protection. Yet economic interests are filtered through a complex political process. The detours, redefinitions, and compromises they make on the way through Congress, the courts, and the cabinet color the ultimate result. Bargaining among self-interested groups and individuals determines government policy, but only after the bargains wend their way through the political labyrinth.

Domestic politics are important to the international economy, for relations among nations are strongly influenced by politics within nations. There is, after all, no international economy in the abstract, no economic no-man's-land in which world trade and payments take place. The international economy is simply the sum of many national economies, and each national economy is subject to powerful domestic political pressures. Developments in foreign trade and investment affect domestic economic and political interests, and these domestic effects can force changes in government policy. The Great Depression of the 1930s and the debt crisis of the 1980s toppled regimes around the world not because the world economy found incumbents wanting, but because the economic collapse threw important domestic groups into opposition.

International financial developments are reflected in national economics and politics, then, through the prism of affected domestic groups. If a wave of foreign defaults threatens the international financial system, banks and bondholders press the government to intervene. If international interest rates skyrocket, companies with debts to foreigners scramble for government policies to relieve the financial pressure on them. If financial integration threatens the profitability of American steel-makers, they demand government insulation and support. International economic trends are filtered through the preferences of domestic groups, who pressure politicians for policies to match their interests.

National responses to international financial developments reflect domestic political bargains; by the same token, many international financial developments themselves have their origin in the domestic politics of the nations that make up the world economy. Simply and schematically put, domestic economic and political developments create the basis for a country's international economic relations. These international economic relations can change the domestic economic environment and thus affect the interests of groups, firms, and individuals inside the nation. Those whose interests are affected can in turn act in the political arena to reinforce or defend their position in the light of the new international economic realities.

This continuous interaction of domestic and international politics and economics is a constant of the world's financial system, and of America's participation in it. The rise of American international banking after 1890 led to important conflicts within the United States over how the government should deal with the new overseas interests of American bankers; the resultant political strife was a major barrier to the further expansion of American international finance. After World War II, domestic political obstacles to American international finance were largely removed, as the Cold War defused much of the historical American wariness of involvement in international affairs. In a congenial domestic and international environment, global banking grew with extraordinary rapidity. Modern international financial markets have become so large and efficient at moving money from place to place that their operations have again become highly politicized. Within the United States, those endangered by international economic integration are once more exerting pressure on the government to restrict the effects, or the activities, of international banking.

The mutual interplay of the international economy and American politics is not new, of course; every turning point in American history has been associated with a transformation of the country's international economic relations. The thirteen colonies' battle for independence was both effect and cause of the decline of British mercantilism. The conflict between the plantation South and the small-farming and urban North was part and parcel of disputes over whether the United States would turn inward in building an industrial society or remain a principal supplier of Europe's raw materials and customer for Europe's manufacturers. The end of American economic insularity fifty years later, during World War I, had domestic ramifications that shook American politics until the 1950s. Time and again, developments in the international economy and in domestic economic relations led to political conflict between groups with divergent interests, and then to a political resolution that set the country on a new course.

Changes in the international economic and political environment indeed gave birth to the American Republic itself. The thirteen colonies were an important source of raw materials and markets for Britain's traders and manufacturers. Imperial policy reinforced the colonies' position as supplier of raw materials and importer of finished goods: the colonists were forbidden to sell many of their exports anywhere but to Great Britain and forced to purchase major imports from Britain. The result was that the British paid artificially low prices for the raw materials they bought from the colonies, while the colonies paid artificially high prices for the products they imported from the homeland.

Trade restrictions were especially onerous for the Virginia

planters of export crops and Boston merchants and shipowners whose economic opportunities were most severely restricted by British mercantilism. Yet British colonialism had many attractions for the early settlers: the mother country provided crucial military protection on both sea and land, especially from French and Spanish settlers to the north, west, and south, and from Indians who often allied themselves with England's European rivals. The burden of British mercantilism was bearable to the colonists so long as its counterpart, British military protection, was essential.

The evolution of the British and colonial economies began to erode support for Britain's colonial mercantilism on both sides of the Atlantic around the middle of the eighteenth century. In the United Kingdom, the Industrial Revolution led much of the growing British manufacturing class to believe, along with Adam Smith, that Britain's industrial edge was great enough to dispense with costly government intervention to maintain closed markets. The publication of Smith's *The Wealth of Nations* in 1776 was an early salvo in the battle to force the Crown to *laissez-faire*—to let businessmen act unencumbered. For Smith, the Edinburgh commissioner of customs, the "always and necessarily hurtful" colonial mercantilist policies were a net loss to the British economy: "The monopoly of the colony trade, therefore, like all the other mean and malignant expedients of the mercantile system, depresses the industry of all other countries, but chiefly that of the colonies, without in the least increasing, but on the contrary diminishing, that of the country in whose favor it was established."[1] As modern industry grew in Great Britain, support for mercantilist restraints on trade waned.

Sentiment in the American colonies also shifted as the colonial economy grew and the political environment changed. The growers and traders of agricultural exports accumulated wealth and power, and the Crown's constraints chafed ever more unbearably. At the same time, military protection had become far less urgent. The 1763 British victory in the Seven Years' War, known in North America as the French and Indian War, swept the French from the continent; although Spain claimed much of the area west of the Mississippi, Spain was already weak. The colonies were increasingly unwilling to give away their economic autonomy for military protection of dubious importance, while the British were increasingly unconvinced that mercantilist economic policies were working well enough to justify costly colonial military expenditures. The British tried to force the colonies to pay for their own defense even as the colonists needed this defense less, for British military success had made British military protection redundant. Against the backdrop of growing dissatisfaction with British mercantilism in both the colonies and Great Britain, anticolonial sentiment deepened in its traditional Boston and Virginia strongholds, spread to other areas, and erupted into the American War of Independence.

Beginning in the 1820s, the new nation's international economic relations fueled an extraordinary cotton export boom with major domestic political implications. Britain's industrialization, especially in cotton textiles, dramatically increased its demand for raw cotton, while the cotton gin allowed southern soil to be turned over to the cultivation of short-staple cotton to supply British mills. Plantation agriculture, and the slavery on which it rested, became one of the country's economic dynamos. The southern United States grew into prototypical neocolonial status, selling raw materials to and buying finished goods from Great Britain. British capital complemented its trade, financing the construction of canals, railroads, and port facilities to bring the cotton to market.

The cotton South was drawn into Britain's economic orbit, but northern industries competed fiercely with their British counterparts. The political strife that ensued tore the country apart. In a pattern that has since been repeated in virtually every other developing nation, the United States split between those tied to traditional exports and those concerned with protecting and developing the home market. Southern plantation agriculture wanted to maintain its close ties to British industry and finance, and opposed high tariffs that would keep cheap British goods out of the U.S. market. The industrializing areas of the North viewed Britain as their principal rival, and called for stringent tariff protection. This conflict was overlain on the collision of slave plantation agriculture and free farming, both fighting for the fertile Midwest and Great Plains; a series of regional, moral, and constitutional debates complicated the cleavage. If the origins of the clash were in large part economic, it became a more and more political dispute as the two sides contended for control of the three branches of government. Admissions to the Union, judicial appointments and decisions, and presidential nominations were all caught up in the sectional standoff until the potential for compromise was exhausted and war broke out.

From the Civil War onward, the United States devoted its energies first and foremost to industrial development. The result was something akin to an internal version of British mercantilism, as the country's westward expansion was used to build its industrial base. High tariffs on manufactured products kept American prices for finished goods high. Yet, since trade in agricultural products was generally free, farm prices were held to world market levels. Thus farm earnings (and urban food prices) were held down while industrial goods were relatively expensive. In addition, farm prices were subject to great fluctuations that left heavily indebted farmers unable to meet their financial obligations. While manufacturing boomed, agricultural performance was decidedly uneven and economic conditions were precarious for much of the farm sector.

Rural resentment of the pro-industrial bias of American economic policy flared into farm-belt radicalism throughout the sixty years before World War I. As world grain prices fell in the late 1800s, grain-belt antipathy to the urban-based robber barons, bankers, and railroad men found fertile soil in the Greenback Populism that Democrat William Jennings Bryan tried to harvest in his 1896, 1900, and 1908 presidential campaigns. The farmers wanted to get the country off the gold standard and onto a joint gold-silver standard that would expand the money supply. Bryan's famous plea not to "crucify mankind upon a cross of gold" was, in less florid terms, a call for price inflation to raise farm prices and reduce the real value of farmers' debts. Bryan consistently swept the rural Southeast, did very well on the Great Plains, and attracted the Rocky Mountain states with the prospect of greater demand for their silver output.

The agrarian Populists and Socialists were unable to slow the dazzling advance of American industry. By the 1880s, the United States was the world's leading industrial power, and the self-absorbed onrush of industrialization created the modern American political and social system. Millions of immigrants flooded into the industrial centers. The labor movement grew, was repressed, then grew again. The political system settled into the two-party pattern it retains today, while federal, state, and local governments began to develop the bureaucratic appurtenances of a modern state. The process went on nearly self-contained, as the United States practically withdrew from world politics and curtailed its participation in the world economy.

In the 1890s, however, a transformed America began to

emerge from its international economic isolation. American industry was now powerful and, in some lines at least, able to hold its own in world markets. American statesmen went about trying to secure access to these markets, even as they battled to carve out a place for the United States in Europe's rush for colonies and influence.

American international banking began around the turn of the century, as politicians, military men, and businessmen came together to thrust the United States outward. Before the 1890s, Wall Street had been preoccupied with financing American agricultural and industrial development. Eventually, the bankers began to look for new business abroad, financing the country's growing foreign trade and eventually lending money to foreigners. From 1898 until 1914, the United States gradually extended its influence, especially to the Caribbean Basin and China. Yet the United States remained both politically and economically self-absorbed until its burgeoning international economic and political ties drew it into World War I.

The First World War and its aftermath pulled the United States into the world economy with a vengeance. Wall Street became banker to the world, and American corporations set up shop all over Europe and Latin America. Nonetheless, the size of the American market and the insularity of American politics tempered the enthusiasm of many Americans for international adventures. The American political system was torn between "internationalists" who wanted the United States to tap its potential for world economic and political leadership, and "isolationists" content to steer clear of European entanglements and rely on America's traditional sphere of influence. After a brief flurry of Wilsonian engagement, the country beat a partial retreat during the 1920s and stayed out of the international political arena as much as possible—even as American bankers came to dominate the world economy.

The twin traumas of the Depression and World War II decided the debate over American international involvement. The initial impact of the Depression drove the American pendulum all the way back toward isolation. In 1930, Congress raised tariffs to historic highs, and shortly thereafter the international monetary and financial system collapsed. The early Roosevelt administration concentrated on getting the domestic economy going again. In the late 1930s, however, Roosevelt jettisoned economic isolationism in favor of a commitment to American international economic leadership.

The United States climbed out of Depression and into World War II with a restored belief in the American destiny to reshape global politics and economics. After World War II, American finance and industry led the capitalist world toward economic integration. American multinational corporations spread over the globe, and soon multinationals from Western Europe and Japan followed suit. The world's leading banks built an enormous offshore financial system that moves tens of billions of dollars around the world every hour. As the world's industrial economies became more and more open, and as postwar prosperity began to tail off in the 1970s, the domestic and international political arrangements worked out in the 1930s and 1940s began to fall apart. The New Deal coalition in the United States was one such casualty, as the urban and industrial working-class core of the Democratic party shrank with the decline of American basic industry.

Throughout American history, international economic relations have been a major source of political strife between the various domestic interests created as the country has grown. The evolution of British mercantile policy in the mid-1700s drove colonial planters and traders to rebellion as their needs clashed with those of the metropolis. From the

1820s on, the expansion of the country's cotton trade with Britain threw the free-trade plantation South into growing conflict with northern industry and free farming, until the Civil War decided the question. After 1870, inward-looking industrialization under protective tariffs drove a wedge between urban and rural America and called forth successive waves of unsuccessful farm movements all through the late nineteenth and early twentieth centuries. The dramatic overseas expansion of American finance and industry during and after World War I called forth an isolationist reaction that nearly immobilized American foreign policy until the late 1930s. Changes in the international economic orientation of the United States have been accompanied by such major domestic social upheavals as the Revolution, the Civil War, and the Depression.

The next ten years will be a watershed in American politics and economics, comparable to if somewhat less dramatic than these previous episodes. The evolution of the country's interaction with the world economy is driving much of the change, as the United States splits into camps favored and injured by the globalization of finance and trade. The outcome of the conflict will determine America's position in the world, and the overwhelming economic size of the United States means that current trends in American society will shape the rest of the world for years to come. The world's economies may be drawn ever closer into a swirling mass of relentless market pressures, or they may shatter into hostile blocs. The outcome will affect every company and politician, every worker and consumer, in the United States.

This book explains the background of contemporary conflicts over American international finance, and analyzes possible paths to the future. It focuses on America's international bankers, who have been at the center of America's international economic position for over fifty years, and who will be crucial actors in future political debates.

Banking on the World contains no sweeping forecasts or precise predictions. The future depends on the interaction of far too many variables to allow for confident projections. Yet there are clear indications of the crucial issues and interests that will define the debates to come, and of the principal people who will decide the outcome of these conflicts.

The starting point for analyzing the present and the future of American international finance is understanding the past. The contemporary role of the United States in the world financial system is the result of a long history of American international banking. The initial overseas expansion of America's international bankers started in the 1890s and ran through the 1920s, and most of today's issues have their roots in this earlier period.

A constant and central feature of the politics of American international finance is the great ambivalence of many in the United States about international economic integration, even as the U.S. government and American businesses have led the world toward global markets. Perhaps the most striking example of this tension was in the 1920s and 1930s, when American "internationalists" did constant battle with "isolationists" over the nation's economic and political relations with the rest of the world. These conflicts shaped the environment within which American international bankers tried after World War I to drive the United States toward international financial leadership. We begin, then, by going back to the formative years of American international banking, an exhilarating and frustrating time in which Wall Street rose meteorically to command the world economy, then saw the international financial system collapse under the weight of depression, default, and eventually war.

2

The Early Years of American International Banking

The United States became a world financial power during and after World War I. The war and its aftermath drew the country's major banks into international lending in unprecedented amounts, for the United States was a capital-rich country in a capital-starved world. In the 1920s, foreign loans were immensely popular on Wall Street, and America's leading financial institutions developed important economic interests in Europe, Latin America, and Asia. As their interests became more international, the bankers pressured the U.S. government for policies in line with their global concerns.

Within the United States, however, there was great resistance to American political involvement in foreign affairs. The U.S. economy was still very heavily oriented toward the domestic market; the rest of the world economy was, if anything, more of a threat than an opportunity for most economic interests. Many Americans also felt that the country's brief involvement in European affairs during World War I was more than enough, and yearned for a return to the days when the United States was blissfully apart from the rest of the world's incessant bickering.

Political opposition within the United States thus made it impossible for American international bankers to achieve all that they wanted in the inter-war years. The bitter experience with domestic hostility to their efforts made American international financiers painfully aware of how much their international economic success depended on domestic political support.

The United States is a relative newcomer to international banking. When Americans began lending overseas in the 1890s, the Dutch and British already had centuries of international financial experience behind them, and the French and Germans were nearly as seasoned. Nevertheless, American bankers were the world's leading lenders by the end of World War I, just a few years after they first burst upon the international scene. This exhilarating rise to world financial supremacy was, however, marred by a series of frustrating setbacks that culminated in the Great Depression of the 1930s.

For its first hundred years, the United States mattered in international finance only as a borrower—indeed, the United States was the major international borrower of the 1800s. In the early days of the Republic, when Amsterdam was the world's financial center, the struggling American government regularly turned to the Dutch for funds; by 1796, the new country's debt to Dutch investors was twice as large as federal government spending. The Dutch bankrolled Alexander Hamilton's Society for the Useful Promotion of Manufactures, dedicated to establishing American industry and responsible for the development of the country's first planned industrial town in Paterson, New Jersey. The new nation was so short of capital that by 1809 foreigners even owned three-quarters of the stock of America's first central bank. As the country grew, capital poured in from abroad, although in the meantime Britain wrested world financial leadership from Holland. British investors financed canals, shipping lines, railroads, warehouses, and other ventures to get American agricultural products and raw materials to Europe, and to open the western frontier.

Many of the country's leading financial houses first achieved recognition as conduits for the foreign capital that the developing United States was sucking in. August Belmont was the Rothschilds' representative in America. Morgan; Kidder, Peabody; Brown Brothers; J. and W. Seligman; and Kuhn, Loeb functioned primarily as channels to draw loans into the United States from the world's financial centers in London, Paris, and Hamburg.

The fortunes of America's most famous financial family, the Morgans, typified the country's international economic trajectory. In 1854, Junius Spencer Morgan, a New England merchant, moved to London to manage and finance American trade with Europe. Shortly after, Morgan's son John Pierpont became his father's representative on Wall Street. The House of Morgan, headed by its London office, rapidly carved out an important position selling the stocks and bonds of American corporations, and of the state and federal governments, to European investors. The family further strengthened its position by an 1871 alliance with the important Philadelphia bank of Drexel and Company, which added a Paris branch to the institution's network and allowed the firm to sell American securities to investors on the Continent.

In the 1880s, however, the United States ceased to be a major net borrower abroad. By then the big northeastern banks controlled an important financial market of their own, for banks all over the United States held their reserves and excess funds in New York. Money flowed to New York, said bitter contemporaries, like water flowing downhill. The pools of capital that accumulated in New York gave the arbiters of that market great power in the nation's economy.

The big New York commercial and investment banks were ideally positioned to help organize and finance the major railroad, mining, agribusiness, and manufacturing combines that led American industry past the British by 1885.

Once more, the Morgan firm was in the forefront of the nation's shift from a major borrower to an economic power in its own right. In the late 1870s, the center of the house's gravity began to shift away from its London and Paris branches and toward New York, where J. P. Morgan was increasingly important as an independent financial force. Although the firm continued to raise money from British, French, and German investors, J. P. Morgan rapidly positioned himself at the center of America's growing industry. His ties with the likes of Andrew Carnegie, Cornelius Vanderbilt, Jay Gould, and Thomas Edison involved him in financing and running most of the country's major railroads—the New York Central, Erie, Reading, Baltimore and Ohio, Chesapeake and Ohio, Northern Pacific, and Great Northern, among others—along with such industrial firms as General Electric and U.S. Steel. By the time Junius Morgan died in Europe in 1890, his son J. P. was America's most powerful banker. Junius prospered by linking powerful European investors with American borrowers, while J. P. dominated Wall Street by serving as an intermediary among major American businessmen themselves.

As the economic might of the United States grew and the country weaned itself of foreign capital, American investors began to look abroad for profit opportunities. In the 1880s and 1890s the province of Quebec borrowed on Wall Street, Junius Morgan bankrolled Cecil Rhodes' African diamond mines, the firm of Kuhn, Loeb financed Mexican railroad building, and J. P. Morgan backed telegraph developers in Mexico and reorganized the finances of Mexican dictator Porfirio Díaz. By the late 1890s, American bankers, along with their clients in mining, agribusiness, and industry, were seriously interested in building spheres of economic influence overseas.

The turnaround of America's international financial position in the last years of the nineteenth century was part and parcel of a general attempt by the country's economic and political leaders to secure for the United States a more prominent place in world affairs. Industrialists were eager to increase their exports, especially after the depression of 1893–1897 convinced the big manufacturing combines that, with America's open spaces filled, foreign markets were all that could assure continued economic expansion. The bankers and traders who had long worked with the industrialists shared the appetite of their industrial clients for overseas business. The bankers, traders, and industrialists found ready allies in a new school of American politicians who wanted the United States to project its power internationally. This "power school," led by Theodore Roosevelt, John Hay, Henry Cabot Lodge, and Elihu Root, had great plans to pull the United States into the thick of world politics. Senator Albert Beveridge of Indiana, typical of what Mark Twain called "the Blessings-of-Civilization Trust," said in 1898· "American factories are making more than the American people can use, American soil is producing more than they can consume. Fate has written our policy for us; the trade of the world must and shall be ours. . . . Our institutions will follow our flag on the wings of commerce."[1]

American politicians, industrialists, bankers, and traders interested in world power and markets faced serious obstacles on the path to prominence. While the United States was consumed in its Civil War and in "clearing" the frontier, Europe had divided most of Asia and Africa into colonial preserves. The China trade, the pride of Boston and San Francisco merchants, was endangered by the carving up of

China into exclusive spheres managed by the Europeans and Japanese. South America traded primarily with England, and European influence was supreme even in the Caribbean.

It was clear to the would-be empire builders that the United States could not be a world power if it did not control its Caribbean backyard and the canal that everyone knew would eventually be built to connect the Atlantic with the Pacific. Much of America's export trade depended on free transit through the Caribbean from southern ports, and from a military standpoint the Gulf Coast was the country's soft underbelly. Similarly, no power could be truly great that was excluded from the scramble for China. Not only was the China trade a traditional American stronghold, but inclusion in the management of Chinese affairs would be a sign that the other imperial powers took the United States seriously.

In the last years of the century, then, the United States began building a great navy—and an empire to go with it. The Philippines and Guam were taken from Spain; along with Hawaii and Samoa, which were annexed at much the same time, they gave America a beachhead in the Orient. Spain also provided two strategic prizes in the Caribbean: Cuba and Puerto Rico. Five years later, Teddy Roosevelt "took Panama," as he later boasted, by fomenting a separatist rebellion in Colombia's northernmost province. The new nation of Panama conveniently and immediately agreed to sign an American canal treaty where the Colombians had balked.

In 1904, Roosevelt issued what came to be known as the Roosevelt Corollary to the Monroe Doctrine, asserting the right of the United States—and of no other power—to maintain order in the Western Hemisphere. "Chronic wrongdoing" by native populations, said TR, might "ultimately require intervention by some civilized nation." In Latin

America, "the Monroe Doctrine may force the United States, however reluctantly . . . to the exercise of an international police power."[2] Despite the bluster, American designs were largely confined to the Caribbean, where local regimes were weak and the Europeans indifferent. They probably felt the same sense of inevitability as did Secretary of War Elihu Root in 1905: "The inevitable effect of our building the Canal must be to require us to police the surrounding premises. In the nature of things, trade and control, and the obligation to keep order which go with them, must come our way."[3]

The formula for America's assertion of its "trade and control, and the obligation to keep order" in its Caribbean "premises" involved the close cooperation of statesmen and bankers. The Europeans' right to intervene was often predicated on their need to collect local debts. The United States removed this pretext simply by having American bankers buy out the Europeans. From then on, the only legitimate interventions were American. Where lucrative, American investors carved out plantations, or mines, or railroads. In case of "chronic wrongdoing" American troops were available.

American investors built up sugar holdings in Cuba, Puerto Rico, the Dominican Republic, Mexico, and elsewhere. The National City Bank of New York (precursor of Citibank) bought the National Bank of the Republic of Haiti and the nation's railroad system. American bankers made stabilization loans—usually in concert with U.S. military occupation and financial control—to Cuba, the Dominican Republic, Haiti, Nicaragua, and other nations in and around the Caribbean. In addition to the "special relationship" with Cuba, Puerto Rico, and Panama, American troops occupied Haiti from 1915 to 1934, the Dominican Republic from 1916 to 1924, and Nicaragua from 1912 to 1933, with a brief withdrawal in 1925.

American bankers worked hand in hand with resident investors, American exporters, and the empire builders in government to consolidate American control of the Caribbean. In China at much the same time, many of the same Americans were fighting their way into the world's most hotly contested market.

By the turn of the twentieth century the Chinese Empire was falling apart. Both cause and consequence of its collapse was a rush on the part of the European powers and Japan to stake claims for the inevitable clearance sale. Exclusive spheres of influence were established, and most excluded of all were American businessmen. Despite Secretary of State Hay's Open Door Notes of 1899 and 1901, calling for equal access to the China trade, the United States was being frozen out. Most alarming, it was being ignored in two economically and politically important facets of foreign endeavor: railroad building and finance.

Willard Straight, a young friend of railroad man Edward Harriman and of President Theodore Roosevelt, meant to rectify America's subordinate position in China. In 1906 he became American Consul to Mukden (now Shenyang), a major industrial center in Manchuria, four hundred miles northeast of Peking. Mukden was at the center of intrigue among the foreign powers, and Straight was eager to enter the fray. A follower of the "power school," Straight was an impassioned believer in what both detractors and supporters were coming to call Dollar Diplomacy—the simultaneous foreign expansion of American financial and political power. For Straight, indeed, politics and business were "in reality but different expressions of interests which are fundamentally the same."[4]

Almost as soon as he arrived in Manchuria, Straight began to organize the entry of American capital into the race for China. He circumvented the hostile American Ambassador in Beijing and directly contacted Secretary of State Elihu Root and Secretary of War William Howard Taft to secure the backing of the U.S. government for American loans to China.

In 1909, Straight succeeded in putting together an "American group" of J. P. Morgan; the National City Bank; the First National Bank of New York; the firm of Kuhn, Loeb; and Edward Harriman to fight its way into Chinese railroad finance. Straight resigned his consular position and represented the American group as it negotiated with its European rivals for a share of the Chinese government's business and favor. By 1910, with the help of a threatening telegram from Taft, now president, to the Chinese regent, the American financiers were admitted to the club. A year later, British, French, German, Russian, Japanese, and American bankers signed a loan contract with the new reform government. "Dollar diplomacy," said Straight, "is justified at last." The United States had cracked the European monopoly of Chinese finances.[5]

In fact, the Chinese victory was hollow. Even as the first loan with U.S. participation was being negotiated, China erupted in a nationalist revolution that unsettled the nation for forty years. America got its foot in the Chinese door just as the palace crumbled; yet the principle involved, that America was now a political and financial power to be reckoned with, was as important as the profits foregone.

American bankers were indeed of increasing international importance. The firm of Kuhn, Loeb and the National City Bank, in concert with British and German partners, lent $410 million to Japan during the Russo-Japanese war of 1904–1905. Jacob Schiff—head of Kuhn, Loeb, America's leading Jewish investment bank—was especially pleased to be able to assist the Japanese war against the anti-Semitic "enemy of mankind" sitting in St. Petersburg. The British government itself borrowed some $200 million from the firms of both Morgan and Kidder, Peabody between 1900 and 1902 to help finance the expensive Boer War.

Indeed, J. P. Morgan had become as prominent in Europe as in America. His financial prowess was of course unchallenged; his stabilization of the crisis of 1895 and the panic of 1907 was legend, as was his 1901 organization of the steel trust. Morgan was an international figure in the cultural realm as well; he had lived much of his early life in Europe and hardly conformed to the common European image of the provincial American millionaire. Morgan was an impressive art collector, was president of the Metropolitan Museum of Art from 1904 until 1913, and spent half of what he earned amassing one of the world's great collections. Morgan's frequent trips to Europe excited both fascination and concern with the growing power of the United States. As Senator Mark Hanna remarked sardonically during one of Morgan's stays in England, "I wouldn't be surprised to hear he was getting up a syndicate to buy the British Empire. It isn't safe as long as he's over there."[6]

American economic influence was on the rise. In 1902, Secretary of State John Hay proclaimed happily that "the financial center of the world, which required thousands of years to journey from the Euphrates to the Thames and Seine, seems passing to the Hudson between daybreak and dark."[7] On the military and diplomatic side, the United States impressed much of the world with the round-the-globe jaunt of the Great White Fleet in 1907.

Yet the United States was still a minor financial power. On the eve of World War I, all outstanding American foreign loans totaled less than a billion dollars; London's City lent that much overseas in a single year. By 1914, British investors were owed some $20 billion by foreigners, French financiers held $10 billion in foreign loans, and the Germans another $5 billion. America's rise to financial power was going slowly. But when J. P. Morgan died in 1913, his successor, J. P. Morgan, Jr.—Jack, as he was known—had no idea that within a matter of months World War I would catapult the Morgan firm into the center of international finance.

When World War I broke out in August 1914, the world's financial markets panicked. For a century international trade and finance had been managed from London's City, largely in pounds sterling. British bankers and British traders were pillars of the world economy, but they could not conduct business as usual under wartime conditions. In a matter of weeks European financial markets closed, and even those that eventually reopened were hopelessly crippled. Within six months Wall Street—which itself had only narrowly averted panic—was the world's only fully functional financial market.

By early 1915, American bankers had realized that war in Europe opened up immense possibilities. "The reversal in our financial position," said Chairman Alexander Hemphill of the Guaranty Trust Company, "has been . . . little less than revolutionary." The war "marked the creation of a new epoch in international finance, especially for the United States."[8]

The key to this revolution lay in Europe's desperate need for American food and munitions. The belligerents had expected a short and decisive war, and were economically unable to sustain the drain on their resources as the fighting bogged down. The European war also cut off the Latin American countries, and even some of Europe's own colonies, from previous sources of manufactured goods. The result on both fronts was a sustained and unprecedented boom in American exports, and in American industry. In the three years of the war preceding U.S. entry, the American trade surplus ran at over five times prewar levels; by 1916, American munitions manufacturers were exporting $1.3 billion a year, up from $40 million in 1914.

Most of the American exports to Europe went to Great Britain and France, since Germany and its allies were effectively blockaded. The British and French paid for some of the American food and weapons by selling back to the United States some $2 billion of their American investments, but this was not enough.

The British and French could only continue to buy from the United States if American banks lent them the money to do so. Despite an early commitment to economic as well as diplomatic neutrality, the Wilson administration soon decided that trade with the Allies was too important to be sacrificed to dubious principles. As Treasury Secretary William McAdoo told Wilson, his father-in-law, about the Allied trade, "to maintain our prosperity we must finance it. Otherwise it may stop and that would be disastrous."[9] In August 1915, the administration agreed to allow private American loans to the Allies, and in October J. P. Morgan and Company floated a $500 million loan to the British and French governments.

By the time the United States entered the war, its private financiers had lent some $2.6 billion to Britain, France, and their allies. Most of the lending was managed by Morgan, which also acted as the American purchasing agent for the Allies. Morgan's purchases on behalf of its Allied clients averaged over a billion dollars a year between 1914 and 1917, and accounted for one-quarter of all American exports. We can get an idea of the magnitude involved by noting that the $2.6 billion in lending between 1914 and 1917 was more than twice the federal government's debt at the time, while Morgan's purchases for the Allies were greater than 1910 federal government spending. More generally, since the

U.S. economy today is about one hundred times as large as it was at the time of World War I, owing to both inflation and economic growth, we might multiply the figures by 100 to get a sense of their present-day equivalents.

While the financial benefits to Morgan's are obvious—the firm's assets more than doubled between 1914 and 1917—America's leading financial institution also felt that its activities were preparing the way for the United States to join England in world financial leadership. America's bankers knew, by the second year of the war, that they would henceforth be central players in world politics. Thomas Lamont, one of Morgan's most influential partners, was realistic, if flowery, in 1915: "When that terrible, blood-red fog of war burns away we shall see finance still standing firm. We shall see the spectacle of the business men of all nations paying to one another their just debts. . . . We shall see finance standing ready to develop new enterprises; to find money to till new fields; to help rebuild a broken and wreck-strewn world; to set the fires of industry blazing brightly again and lighting up the earth with the triumphs of peace."[10]

American bankers also moved in on the Europeans' lucrative banking business in Latin America and the Far East. The new Federal Reserve System, set up immediately before the war, greatly improved American financiers' international competitiveness; among other things, the Federal Reserve Act allowed nationally chartered banks to establish foreign branches for the first time. In 1914, under the new Fed, the National City Bank of New York (later Citibank) set up its first overseas branch, in Buenos Aires. By the end of the war, National City Bank had eighteen foreign branches, fifteen in Latin America. By 1926, National City Bank had eighty-four branches, American Express had forty-seven, and a smattering of other banks had twenty-three. The big American banks were not only financing the European powers, for the first time they were competing with them in trade finance in Latin America and parts of Asia.

The more the Allies borrowed, the more the British themselves became uncomfortably aware that international economic leadership was slipping away from them. The chairman of an October 1916 British interministerial conference to consider alternatives to reliance on the United States reported glumly that "there was really nothing to deliberate about. . . . American supplies are so necessary to us that reprisals, while they would produce tremendous distress in America, would also practically stop the war." A young Treasury official, John Maynard Keynes, was categorical in reporting to the British Cabinet: "The sums which this country will require to borrow in the United States of America in the next six to nine months are so enormous, amounting to several times the national debt of that country, that it will be necessary to appeal to every class and section of the investing public. . . . It is hardly an exaggeration to say that in a few months' time the American executive and the American public will be in a position to dictate to this country on matters that affect us more dearly than them."[11]

In March 1917, indeed, Morgan's firm told the British Treasury that private lending was no longer feasible. At much the same time, however, the Germans, in a serious miscalculation, resumed unlimited submarine warfare. The ensuing American declaration of war, on April 4, 1917, came just in time to save Allied finances. The U.S. government replaced the private bankers, issued five series of war bonds, and lent $9.6 billion to the Allies between May 1917 and April 1919.

The Allies had become America's financial dependents. Great Britain, the world's greatest lender five years earlier, was deeply in debt to the United States. Wilson was confident of the consequences, and wrote to Colonel E. M. House in July 1917: "When the war is over we can force them [the British] to our way of thinking, because by that time they will, among other things, be financially in our hands."[12]

America emerged from World War I as the globe's new superpower. Even as Europe destroyed itself, American manufacturing production went from $23 billion in 1914 to $60 billion in 1919. Private American overseas loans went from $1 billion to $3 billion, and the Allies owed another $10 billion to the U.S. government. American statesmen and businessmen were in a new position, as Wilson put it: "We have got to finance the world in some important degree, and those who finance the world must understand it and rule it with their spirits and with their minds."[13]

World War I put American international bankers at the center of world politics, and they faced the aftermath of World War I with great enthusiasm. In the years following the war, the financiers became unarguably the greatest economic force in international relations. Yet their ambitious plans for a postwar world congenial to their interests were continually waylaid by political opponents within the United States, who made it very difficult for the U.S. government to back up U.S. bankers overseas. As Woodrow Wilson discovered in his unsuccessful fight for the United States to join the League of Nations, it was far easier to have one's way with war-weary Europe that it was to win over the representatives of America's heartland in Washington.

The nation's international financiers, though, saw clearly the course they wanted to follow. The time had come for America "to seize and hold her rightful heritage—the material and moral leadership in world affairs," in the words of New York financier A. J. Rosenthal. Otto Kahn of Kuhn, Loeb told his countrymen: "Whether we like it or not we must take part in the economic affairs of Europe."[14] This meant supervising European reconstruction—and, if necessary, financing it. James Sheldon of Lee, Higginson expressed in 1920 the general belief of his colleagues on Wall Street that "we must contrive to continue selling abroad or look forward to industrial depression." In Europe's devastated state, sales could only be on credit. Sheldon continued, "If this country can contrive the means of granting credit to our former allies, they can continue to buy from us. . . . By lending well within the limits of safety we can place Europe upon a basis of profitable production within a comparatively short time."[15]

American bankers' participation in planning for the postwar settlement began as soon as the United States entered the war. Thomas Lamont, the prominent Morgan partner, sailed to Europe in the autumn of 1917 as a confidential financial adviser to the all-important mission of Colonel E. M. House to discuss wartime and postwar plans with the British and French. After the Armistice, Lamont once more set off for Europe. This time he was an official U.S. Treasury representative to the complex negotiations at the Paris Peace Conference. Lamont and fellow Wall Streeters Norman H. Davis, Bernard Baruch, and a young John Foster Dulles spent most of the first half of 1919 working on the crucial economic components of the Versailles treaty. The Americans were especially concerned to moderate the Anglo-French demands that Germany pay exorbitant war reparations, in excess of $100 billion; they eventually obtained an acceptable reparations agreement, although one still too punitive and imprecise for Lamont.

After the Versailles negotiations were over, the bankers returned to the private sector, but continued their efforts at international crisis management. As Thomas Lamont later put it, Wall Street held Europe together in the 1920s: "Bad as were the economic and financial conditions in Europe following World War I, nevertheless they were sufficiently within control to be handled largely by private banking and investment interests."[16]

During the 1920s, United States private bankers initiated, supervised, and funded most of the central developments in the world economy. They built international organizations, stabilized currencies, and oversaw government economic programs in Europe and Latin America. Decision making in the 1920s international economy centered on Wall Street; the United States was a crucial component of the decisions taken; and the world operated in large part on a dollar standard.

When, for example, the economies of Central and Eastern Europe nearly collapsed in the early 1920s, stabilization programs were worked out, funded, and overseen by American and British bankers, generally joined by the Federal Reserve Bank of New York, the Bank of England, and the Financial Committee of the League of Nations. The combined influence of the major New York and London bankers, the world's leading central bankers, and the League of Nations was used to halt economic disintegration, stop the spread of social discontent that was strengthening Communist movements, and put new backbone into Europe's discredited governments and business communities. Wall Street and London demonstrated confidence in the future with large loans to the reorganized governments and generous advice on how to use the borrowed funds to restore normal business conditions.

The first collaborative loan was to Austria in 1923, where hyperinflation had come close to destroying the economy; success in Austria was followed by a series of stabilization loans to Belgium, Italy, Poland, and Rumania. In all these cases, Wall Street led negotiations, set conditions, and then—along with the New York Fed and the Bank of England—supervised compliance.

The real test of the bankers' abilities was in reviving a Germany beset by economic uncertainty, hyperinflation, and powerful Communist and Socialist labor movements. The German weak link in the chain of European reconstruction was being weakened still further by persistent French demands for reparations, which they justified by pointing to the French need to repay wartime debts to the American government. Negotiations to rescue the German economy went on for over a year. The principal members of the American delegation were Owen Young of General Electric; Charles Dawes, a Chicago banker long allied with the Morgan firm, and, of course, the Morgan partners. In April 1924, the German package was complete, and Morgan proudly managed the lion's share of the $200 million stabilization loan, a task Jack Morgan called "the most important and responsible job we have had to tackle since the end of 1915."[17]

The Dawes Plan, as it came to be known, was an ingenious example of private American business's attempts to resolve Europe's economic and political conflicts. Morgan arranged the Dawes loan; the resident superintendent of Germany's compliance was an American friendly to Morgan; and the success of the plan depended on continued American lending to Germany. As Shepard Morgan of the Chase National Bank said a few years later of the plan, "its general interest, of course, was to reestablish Germany as a going concern. . . . But its broader consequence was the restoration of confidence, which opened the way for the reestablishment of German credit and the rehabilitation of German industry and trade."[18]

The Dawes Plan was a major victory for postwar stabilization. "At last," said Morgan's Thomas Lamont, "one corner has been turned. Economically Europe seems to be headed in the right direction." It was, said Lamont, "the first bridge built firm enough for all the Allies to march across, shoulder to shoulder."[19]

Marching across the bridge to Germany right after the Allies came a massive flow of American capital. In the six years after the Dawes Plan went into effect, Americans lent over $1.2 billion to Germany and another $1.4 billion to other European nations. At the same time, investment in Europe by American nonfinancial businesses grew so rapidly that in the 1920s many Europeans complained, not for the last time, of an invasion of American multinational corporations. Total direct American investment in Europe went from $200 million before World War I to $1.4 billion in 1929. The German economy relied heavily on American loans, since Wall Street accounted for half of the country's foreign borrowing, while foreign capital as a whole financed a third of all investment in the German economy. Postwar reconstruction and prosperity all over Central and Eastern Europe was sustained by injections of American capital.

America's international bankers after World War I also went about building a network of decision makers and opinion leaders inside the United States sympathetic to their internationalist views and capable of implementing them. The National City Bank helped American universities introduce foreign trade into their curricula. In 1914, New York University set up the nation's first course sequence on overseas commerce; within a year, seventeen universities had similar programs. The bankers also helped found professional schools for the study of overseas conditions, such as Columbia University's School of International Affairs and Princeton's Woodrow Wilson School. They were instrumental in creating the think tanks and research institutions that have since been at the center of America's foreign policy establishment. The Foreign Policy Association, the League of Nations Association (now the United Nations Association), and the Carnegie Endowment for International Peace were all designed to develop a foreign policy, and foreign policy makers, worthy of America's new international role. The most important of these institutions was the Council on Foreign Relations (CFR), formed right after the end of the war. Morgan's chief counsel was the CFR's first president, and Wall Street was overwhelmingly represented on its board. When the council began publishing the journal *Foreign Affairs* to serve as the center for foreign-policy debate, Morgan's Thomas Lamont arranged for the man who had edited Lamont's *New York Evening Post* to become the first editor of the new journal.

Some important sectors of the U.S. government shared the bankers' visions of world leadership. The State Department was a bastion of internationalism, and Charles Evans Hughes, secretary of state from 1921 to 1925, was extremely sympathetic. The new Federal Reserve System, dominated by Benjamin Strong, the powerful chairman of the Federal Reserve Bank of New York, was a reliable ally. "We feel in New York," Strong told his fellow Fed governors in 1921, "that the general recovery of trade around the world is going to be brought about by our making New York a good market in which the world can borrow money."[20] American international bankers, most of them Republicans, found ready if unusual allies in the Wilsonian Democrats, major aspects of whose world vision they shared. This was so much so that Thomas Lamont, a lifelong Republican, voted Democratic for the first time in the 1920 election—specifically because the Democrats were internationalists, while the Republicans had retreated into relative isolationism.

The economic influence of American bankers was extraordinary in the 1920s, and yet the decade was one of repeated political failure and frustration for them. Ironically, the single biggest hurdle to the their well-laid plans turned out to be within the United States itself. After the internationalist interlude of the war, traditional nationalists quickly reasserted their powerful position in American politics.

Despite the fundamental change in America's international economic position, within a couple of years following the end of World War I most of the bankers' international plans ran into serious opposition within the American political system, and with a few exceptions this opposition blocked their full implementation. This is especially striking since most of the bankers' program—trade liberalization, U.S. aid for European reconstruction, American international monetary and financial leadership—was implemented with little difficulty in the late 1940s. After World War I, however, domestic political opposition to "internationalism," as the new interest in American world leadership came to be called, was so powerful that the bankers and their allies faced round after round of grueling battles and partial defeats in the U.S. Congress and much of the cabinet.

The first major failure of the "internationalists" was the refusal of the U.S. Congress to approve American entry into the League of Nations. Despite some misgivings over Woodrow Wilson's intransigent idealism, most international bankers agreed that the League was a necessary instrument of international cooperation. As Lamont later put it, "America's adhesion to the League, the sacred instrumentality for peace that she herself had proposed, was the world's only chance for thoroughgoing international cooperation and collective security for the preservation of peace."[21]

The League of Nations went down in defeat. Sixty years of accumulated American economic, political, and ideological self-absorption resisted attempts by Woodrow Wilson, the bankers, and other internationalists to commit the U.S. government to a leading role in world politics and economics. For traditional economic nationalists the League of Nations was, as the American Tariff League thundered in 1919, "simply a rally ground for free traders and all who are opposed to the doctrine of 'adequate protection' for the industries and labor of the United States."[22] At a more visceral level, the horrors of World War I had reinforced the unwillingness of many Americans to involve themselves in the affairs of a continent that had proved sickeningly worthy of the charges of moral decadence levied by generations of American Europhobes. "When once the country had turned its back on the League," Lamont recalled bitterly, "it grew more and more cynical as to any value in close international cooperation."[23] Congress voted down virtually all legislation committing the country to the international organizations American bankers had worked so hard to design and implement.

The bankers' second great failure was in their attempt to move the United States away from its traditional protectionism. Unless the United States bought more *from* Europe, the Europeans would not have enough dollars to repay their debts. Otto Kahn told his country: "Having become a creditor nation we have got now to fit ourselves into the role of a creditor nation. We shall have to make up our minds to be more hospitable to imports."[24]

The United States had some of the world's highest trade barriers before World War I, although Woodrow Wilson had brought tariffs down in 1913. The war so disrupted world trade, though, that the effects of these lower tariffs were barely felt. By 1920, a postwar depression had rekindled the debate, and the bankers fought long and hard to keep the American market open to their European clients.

These bankers knew that reducing the American tariff meant giving up some of the domestic market to foreigners, but they saw this as a small price to pay to gain access to foreign markets for American goods and capital. As Norman

H. Davis, a Wall Street banker and Wilson's under secretary of state, insisted, "If we are to continue to lend money to Europe, if we are to be repaid on existing credits, it is to our interest to do all in our power to help Europe in her effort to free herself from this throttling, smothering tangle of artificial trade barriers."[25]

Unfortunately for the free traders, however, there was little support in the United States for tariff reductions. While the big money-center banks, industries such as petroleum and automobiles, and parts of the farm sector (especially Southern export agriculture) were quite international, most of the nation's manufacturers and farmers either faced serious foreign competition or were quite uninterested in foreign markets. The powerful traditional bloc of American industries fearful of foreign competition—the historic core of the Republican party—wanted nothing to do with freer trade. To make matters worse, trade policy was made in a Congress remarkably susceptible to cumulative logrolling that ratcheted tariffs upward as they were negotiated; that is, each Congressman agreed to protect his colleagues' constituencies in return for like consideration for his own.

The tariff, in what A. Barton Hepburn of the Chase National Bank's called an "inexcusable blunder,"[26] was raised in 1921 and 1922. American imports in the 1920s were a lower proportion of the nation's Gross National Product than they had been before World War I, and the protectionists remained extraordinarily powerful in Congress.

The bankers' third major failure was over what soon became known as the "war debts-reparations tangle." By the end of World War I, America's allies were saddled with some $10 billion in war debts to the U.S. government, which they attempted to counterbalance by extracting reparations from a defeated Germany. The European victors complained endlessly about the burden of their payments to the United

States, while Germany deeply resented the ignominy of its reparations payments to the victors. With Europe's economic and political relations hamstrung by war debts and reparations, Europe's capacity to borrow from American bankers and buy from American exporters was seriously limited.

Jack Morgan was blunt: "Those debts should be cancelled," he told the *New York Times* in 1922.[27] The bankers lobbied tirelessly for the United States to write off all or part of Europe's war debts to the U.S. government, which would allow the British and French to scale down their demands for German reparations; the European economies would be sounder, and American lending to Europe would be able to resume. Kuhn, Loeb's Paul Warburg told President Harding in 1921, "It is of infinitely greater value to the United States to reconstruct a world in which we can trade in peace and security than to have on our books obligations of our comrades in arms which they cannot pay."[28]

Yet inside the United States, opposition to canceling Europe's debts to the U.S. government was overwhelming. There was, of course, the "moral" issue: "They hired the money," as Calvin Coolidge said. A more practical objection was that interest on the government's loans to Europe was expected to be about one-seventh of all U.S. government revenue, and a cut in these interest earnings would require a domestic tax increase, which the heartland's industrialists believed would prolong the postwar recession. Their views were supported by the Treasury secretary in the Republican administrations of the 1920s, Andrew Mellon, a Pittsburgh banker with close ties to the domestic steel industry. President Harding, whom Jack Morgan once called a "jelly-fish," concurred. As Thomas Lamont wrote to Morgan with undisguised contempt, Mellon "apparently thinks that in some mysterious way all the indebtedness will finally be paid. He seems to think, too, that if we keep alive all these notes owing to us from dinky little countries all over Europe, the fact that we are holding the notes will give us a sort of strangle hold politically on some of those countries, and enable us to tell them what they shall or shall not do. Herbert Hoover has that same benevolent idea."[29]

Herbert Hoover, Commerce secretary in the post-Wilson administrations and the principal economic policymaker in the cabinet, was himself suspicious of the bankers. Hoover was primarily concerned with American industry, not finance. He wanted American exports to grow, and he wanted the country's industries to have access to the cheap raw materials he had worked to find as a mining engineer abroad. Yet loaning money to the overseas competitors of American business was far less desirable. "A billion dollars spent upon American railways," Hoover insisted, "will give more employment to our people, more advance to our industry, more assistance to our farmers, than twice that sum expended outside the frontiers of the United States."[30]

The result of the international bankers' economic expansion and their frequent political defeat within the United States was a curious patchwork of private involvement in, and public disengagement from, European economic affairs. While Wall Street became more and more committed to the international economy, the U.S. government drew back from Wilsonian internationalism. No American officials participated in international organizations, and American government involvement in European economic affairs was minimal. To be sure, the New York Fed and the State Department cooperated with the bankers, usually in secret; but the executive branch for the most part simply observed while private American bankers tried to reshape the world economy.

Despite their great domestic and international economic

strength, indeed, most of the international bankers' ideas and interests were on the fringes of the American political system in the 1920s. International financiers were, after all, a breed quite apart from most Americans, and even from most American business people; they were likely to know Austria far better than Arkansas. Many of their political initiatives expressed an almost missionary zeal about issues few Americans knew or cared anything about.

Willard Straight, the central player in Dollar Diplomacy in China, was a committed reformer who bankrolled the liberal *New Republic* of Herbert Croly and Walter Lippmann from its inception. After he died of pneumonia in military service in 1918, his widow Dorothy continued to support the magazine for forty years; Dorothy, a Whitney heiress, had unusual enough views on women, labor unions, and world peace that on the occasion of a trip by her to England after World War I the U.S. government cabled the British, "ADVISE DO NOT ALLOW ENTRY TO MRS. WILLARD STRAIGHT. DANGEROUS TROUBLEMAKER."[31] Thomas Lamont, a close friend of Lippmann's was an early and fervent opponent of American hostility to Lenin's revolutionary regime in Russia. His brother and brother-in-law had both been managing editors of the liberal *New York Evening Post;* Lamont himself owned the paper briefly and helped finance the associated *Saturday Review.*

More generally, American international bankers were world-traveling sophisticates with little but contempt for the average government and politician. Jack Morgan frequently complained, as he did in the negotiations on the Dawes loan, how "the politicians have got things in such a state as to add greatly to our difficulties." As the world's leading banker he could avoid the petty squabbles of unprincipled statesmen: "My special job is . . . more fun than being King, Pope, or Prime Minister anywhere—for no one can turn me out of it and I don't have to make any compromises with principles."

The flavor of the Morgan firm's general attitude to government is captured by a story Harold Nicolson tells of a dispute about his biography of Morgan partner Dwight Morrow: "I had written, in describing the immense expansion assumed by Morgan's bank at the outbreak of the war, 'It ceased to be a private firm and became almost a Department of Government.' I meant that as a compliment. Old J. P. Morgan appears to have regarded it as an insult. . . . This is characteristic of both of us. *I* feel it is the highest compliment to compare Morgan's to the Foreign Office. *They* regard it as an insult to suggest that they have any connection with the Government, or any Government. But, you see, the whole point of view is different. I regard bankers and banking as rather low-class fellows. They regard officials as stupid and corrupt."[32] The economic, political, and cultural gulf separating American international bankers from all but a few other American economic and political leaders was yet another obstacle to their plans.

The lenders' inability to control their home base meant that the economic circle remained broken. American tariff policy worked at cross purposes to the bankers by making it difficult for the Europeans to service their debts by selling their goods in the United States. American intransigence on war debts locked Europe into continual economic conflict. American refusal to participate in international organizations impeded the international economic cooperation and coordination that bankers thought was essential.

In the makeshift system devised in the early 1920s, France paid the interest on its U.S. war debts, Germany paid reparations to France, and Wall Street lent to Germany so that German production and exports could be increased to help pay for reparations. The merry-go-round ran until 1928, when a speculative stock market and real estate boom in the United States made foreign lending less attractive. In 1929 the crash demoralized American investors, and in 1930 the astronomical Smoot-Hawley Tariff effectively closed the American market to German and other European exports. By 1933, despite belated attempts by President Hoover to halt the collapse, Germany, Rumania, Bulgaria, Hungary, Greece, Austria, Yugoslavia, Sweden, and Denmark were all in default. Hitler rose to power on the crest of a wave of hatred for the international bankers who had sold Germany into slavery, and panic once again seized Europe.

Even as the financial bubble burst, the American bankers made one last stab at private financial diplomacy. In 1929 Owen Young, Jack Morgan, and Thomas Lamont put together the Young Plan to reduce German reparations, end foreign supervision of the German economy, and establish the Bank for International Settlements (BIS). The BIS would serve, as Chase's Shepard Morgan put it, as "a positive agency of collaboration between central banks and so to further central banking solidarity." It would be a cooperative venture "rid . . . of political entanglements," able to help "relieve credit dislocation, to build a bridge between countries overstocked with capital and those understocked with it."[33]

The last-minute attempts to stave off economic disaster were too late. The Depression ended the international bankers' illusion that they could somehow manage with a partial settlement. If any of them were still unconvinced, the financial crisis of the early 1930s and the wave of defaults that both caused it and resulted from it made clear that the U.S. government could not stand aloof from international financial matters. Ten years later, when the United States got a second chance to rebuild a war-shattered Europe, bankers helped make sure that neither Congress nor the public would stand in the way of a financial *pax Americana.*

Although American bankers were disappointed by the unwillingness of the United States to play a more forceful inter-

national political role in the 1920s, they were quite successful in influencing the development of American policy toward the underdeveloped nations of Latin America. In the
fifteen years after World War I, U.S. diplomacy in the Western Hemisphere evolved slowly toward what Franklin D.
Roosevelt would eventually call the Good Neighbor Policy.
The bankers were central to this evolution.

Two changes in Latin America conditioned U.S. policy.
First, World War I had so absorbed European energies that
by its end, European influence in the hemisphere had been
eclipsed. Even in South America, traditionally a British preserve, American trade and finance came slowly to dominate.
With American paramountcy in the hemisphere secure, the
need for the naked interventionism that had characterized
the earlier Dollar Diplomacy waned. Second, nationalism
was on the rise in Latin America, as elsewhere in the underdeveloped world. As revolutionary nationalism spread from
Mexico, China, and Russia to the Near East, India, and
Africa, bankers and policymakers alike searched for ways, in
the Council on Foreign Relations' words, "to reconcile the
fears of politically weak nations with the need of investment
capital for protection."[34]

The fading of European competition for the hemisphere
encouraged a less frantic search for power and influence,
while the growth of Latin nationalism impelled many government leaders and business people to make concessions to
local conditions. Bankers such as Morgan's Thomas Lamont
concluded that "good faith on the part of a borrower is far
sounder security for a lender than armed forces however
great or powerful. The theory of collecting debts by gunboat
is unrighteous, unworkable, and obsolete."[35]

As they groped their way toward a "good neighborhood,"
the bankers and their State Department allies faced furious
opposition from former friends in the region: the resident
investors. American oil executives, landowners, and sugar

growers in the Caribbean region regarded nationalism as synonymous with Bolshevism, since the first targets of the nationalists were foreign owners of land and natural resources. While the bankers counseled caution, oil executives and planters called continually for armed force. In this case, unlike in Europe, the "softer line" preferred by the bankers prevailed. American policy toward Latin America was less important to most Americans than relations with Europe; once the bankers concentrated their political influence in support of their economic interests in Latin America, what opposition there was turned out to be relatively weak. The two test cases were Cuba and Mexico, and Dwight Morrow was central to both.

Dwight Morrow was a Morgan partner whose expertise was primarily political and diplomatic. As his biographer Harold Nicolson wrote, "He was not a natural banker: by nature he was a statesman. It was indeed a fortunate circumstance which made him a member of a firm to which statesmanship has always seemed more important than routine banking."[36] Morrow was indeed a crafty and well-placed power broker with impressive professional and personal ties; in addition to being a very visible Morgan man, he was an Amherst classmate of Calvin Coolidge, friend of Walter Lippmann, brother to the governor of the Panama Canal Zone, and father-in-law of Charles Lindbergh. Nicolson's biography of Morrow is admiring, but his private notebooks betray a more ambivalent attitude. Frustrated during the course of his research by a never-ending procession of sugary testimonials about Morrow, Nicolson wrote that he was tempted to say, "But this is all nonsense and you know it. Dwight Morrow was a shrewd and selfish little *arriviste* who drank himself to death." Nicolson's summary illustrates both Morrow's power and his flaws: "Morrow is a Protean figure. There was about him a touch of madness, or epilepsy, or something inhuman and abnormal. He had the mind of a super-criminal and the character of a saint. There is no doubt at all that he was a very great man."[37]

Morrow proved his unique abilities, and the viability of the new set of policies the bankers preferred, in Cuba. The island was virtually an American protectorate, its sovereignty hamstrung by its reliance on American sugar interests and by the Platt Amendment to the Cuban Constitution, which gave the United States ultimate legal authority over Cuban affairs. In the 1920s Morrow, along with his fellow Morgan partners Norman Davis and Edward Stettinius, worked to build up the Cuban government as a social force capable of standing on its own. Morrow arranged Morgan loans to Cuba; brought in experts to organize the nation's finances, railroads, and ports; and tutored Cuban dictators on how best to bargain with the U.S. government. Morrow was constantly attacked by the sugar interests, most of whom wanted some form of American annexation; he countered the gunboat school with a call for patience. "Of course," Morrow admitted, "the Government of Cuba has been, and is, very bad. It is possible—yes, it is probable—that the United States might run Cuba much better. As I get older, however, I become more and more convinced that good government is not a substitute for self-government. The kind of mistakes that Americans would make in running Cuba would be different from those that the Cubans themselves make, but they would probably cause a new kind of trouble and a new kind of suffering."[38]

Morrow and his colleagues argued that indirect influence was far more effective than brute force. The most important test of this approach came when Morrow was appointed ambassador to Mexico by Coolidge in 1927. The two countries seemed on the verge of war, especially over Mexican insistence on sovereignty over oil resources claimed by

American oil companies. Secretary of State Frank Kellogg, close to the oil interests, charged that the Mexicans were colluding with the Soviets and with Nicaraguan revolutionaries led by Augusto Cesar Sandino, whom the Marines were unsuccessfully chasing through the hills of Nicaragua, to establish a "Mexican-fostered Bolshevik hegemony intervening between the United States and the Panama Canal."[39]

When Morrow was made ambassador, Mexicans groaned, "first Morrow, then the Marines." But the Morgan man had other plans. He was well acquainted with Mexican affairs; fellow Morgan partner Thomas Lamont chaired the International Committee of Bankers on Mexico, which had been in constant touch with the government for years. Lamont had learned about the Mexicans, he said, that "you could lead them around the world with a lump of sugar but could not drive them an inch," and was contemptuous of those who talk "glibly about wielding the big stick or kicking them in the stomach. There is no big stick to wield and we have no boot that could possibly reach their remote and very tough stomach."[40]

The principal "lumps of sugar" Morrow held were his excellent ties to Americans who could counterbalance the fanaticism of the oil executives. In facing down the oil interests, Morrow called on his Wall Street ties, his friendship with Walter Lippmann, and his considerable negotiating skills. Like Lamont, his willingness to accept the Mexican government as legitimate and as, indeed, the best guarantee of stability in the region, won him the confidence of the postrevolutionary regime. A good dose of public-relations sense made him a popular figure in Mexico—it was on a Morrow-arranged goodwill trip to Mexico that Lindbergh first met Morrow's daughter, whom he married in 1929. Within a few months the major outstanding issues had been settled, and by 1930 Morrow was able to return home to win a Senate seat from New Jersey. (Morrow's promising political career—Lippmann harbored presidential hopes for him—was cut short by his sudden death in 1931.)

By 1930 the "new line" was in place. To be sure, American troops remained in Haiti and Nicaragua, and the United States exercised effective control over the finances of these two nations, along with the Dominican Republic, Cuba, El Salvador, Panama and Bolivia. Yet generally American political and financial influence was far less direct than in the days of Dollar Diplomacy. Lending, trade, and influence had become institutionalized, not dependent on the routine use of force. When Princeton economics professor E. W. Kemmerer went all over Latin America (as well as to Poland, the Philippines, and South Africa) in the 1920s, telling governments how best to run their economies, the governments listened. As Kemmerer himself recognized, the Marines were not needed to win the government's ear: "A country that appoints American financial advisors and follows their advice in reorganizing its finances, along what American investors consider to be the most successful modern lines, increases its chances of appealing to the American investor and of obtaining from him capital on favorable terms."[41]

Between 1919 and 1929, American loans to Latin America more than quadrupled, to $2 billion. By 1929 another $3.5 billion had been invested in Latin America by American nonfinancial corporations in everything from copper mines to automobile factories. For the first time capital flowed to Latin America primarily from the United States, and the American sphere of economic influence included virtually all of the Western Hemisphere.

As in Europe, the Great Depression drove most of the Latin American debtors to the wall; by 1934, over four-fifths of American lending to Latin America was in default. Nevertheless, American policy toward the region had been transformed, and the groundwork had been laid for a new era.

World War I, the 1920s, and the early years of the Great Depression were a time of triumph and frustration for America's international bankers. After 1914, American international finance came of age. It grew to dominate the world economy and to have an important influence on the U.S. foreign policy establishment. In Latin America, finance and foreign policy worked together with little conflict and great success. In Europe, however, every major initiative of the bankers ran up against entrenched political opposition within the United States. The most important elements in the international bankers' plans for the postwar world were defeated. The U.S. government did not lead Europe toward reconstruction; the United States did not open its borders to European goods; the American public did not rally around a new internationalism.

Although America's international bankers were chastened by the outcome of their efforts after World War I, the experience helped them shape a more congenial world after World War II. For one thing, American financial interests abroad grew enormously. In 1914, American loans to foreigners totaled less than a billion dollars and the country was a net debtor; by 1929, foreign debt to American investors was over $8 billion and the United States was the world's principal lender, while direct investments by nonfinancial corporations were another $7.5 billion. Canada and South America had been drawn into America's economic orbit; even Australia and the Dutch East Indies (now Indonesia) were being pulled closer. In Europe, American finance—along with American multinational corporations—had become a force that could make or break governments.

Wall Street built a cohesive network of wealth, power, influence, and intellect in the years after 1914. Individual bankers and their allies accumulated a storehouse of contacts and experience that proved essential during and after World War II. John Foster Dulles, to take one prominent example, cut his teeth on international affairs as a Wall Street lawyer in the 1920s. Among other things, he helped supervise the Polish financial stabilization of 1927 as counsel to the American banks involved (Chase; Blair and Co.; and Bankers Trust). Along with learning about European politics and finances, the experience brought him together with Jean Monnet, Chase's Paris representative, who built the European Common Market during Dulles' reign as U.S. secretary of state in the 1950s.

An entire generation of American foreign-policy makers and shakers, many of them bankers, lawyers for bankers, and financial journalists, formed its view of the world in the turbulence of Versailles, the boom of the 1920s, and the disasters of the 1930s. Much of the powerful cohort of wartime and postwar leaders who would rebuild the world after 1945 came from Wall Street. Dean Acheson, John Foster Dulles, James Forrestal, W. Averell Harriman, Robert Lovett, John McCloy, and Edward Stettinius were all major Wall Street figures who molded American foreign policy after World War II, fired by a determination not to repeat the mistakes of the 1920s.

The veterans of the interwar years believed, first and foremost, that international economic stability demanded determined American leadership. The curious 1920s hybrid of government's official disinterest and banking's economic internationalism was untenable, and must not be repeated. The United States must be the international economic and political leader, and must exercise this leadership to avoid a repetition of the cutthroat chaos of international financial and trade competition in the 1920s and 1930s. Economic interdependence had to be assured, as Norman Davis put it in 1928: "The world has become so interdependent in its economic life that measures adopted by one nation affect the prosperity of others. No nation can afford to exercise its rights of sovereignty without consideration of the effects on others. National selfishness invites international retaliation. The units of the world economy must work together, or rot separately."[42]

As the Depression dragged the nation downward, the stage was set for a new kind of America, and a new kind of American foreign policy. In this new environment the frustrated bankers of the 1920s helped build the new world order of the 1940s.

3

Building the New Order

American international finance was practically dormant in the 1930s and 1940s. By 1936, over three-quarters of all American loans to Latin America, and half of those to Europe, were in default, and the bondholders and debtors did not reach final settlements until the late 1940s and early 1950s. In the meantime, there was no interest in making new loans to the already bankrupt, and all that was left to do on the international financial front was to limit damage and prepare for better days

The international banking business was slow, but American international bankers were anything but inactive. They were powerful people with strong ideas about the proper path for the country to take. In the 1930s and 1940s, American international financiers redoubled their efforts to lead the United States toward a course of action they deemed appropriate. The successive waves of economic, political, and eventually military cataclysms that swept the world after 1930 clearly made it impossible to return to the pattern of the 1920s, in which American international bankers had tried to rebuild the world economy without the committed support of the U.S. government. As Thomas Lamont wrote in 1947, what he and his colleagues in private banking had done in the 1920s, "today can be undertaken only through

the cooperation of governments themselves," for "the chaos
in Europe is so complete that only strong governmental action can hope to reduce it to some degree of order."[1]

The bankers were able to get much of what they wanted
in postwar reconstruction, for domestic resistance to American international economic and political involvement di-
minished in the 1940s. Foreign competitors were few and
far between at the end of World War II. Even so, there was
quite a residue of domestic hostility to internationalism. Perhaps most important in overcoming this hostility was the
connection made within a few years of the war's end between economic internationalism and the broader American
program of building a Western anti-Soviet alliance. On this
basis, despite lingering popular uneasiness about overseas
commitments, America's international bankers were able to
play a central part in building the new international economic order.

The Depression and World War II indeed led the U.S.
government to embrace many of the bankers' ideas, and
many of the bankers themselves, in the process of planning
a postwar world. After the war, the government took on the
task of remaking the international economy, with the enthu-
siastic participation of the bankers in this second chance at
postwar reconstruction. On the basis of the new economic
order that ensued, America's international banks rebuilt
their shattered networks abroad and led the way toward the
largest and most powerful international financial system in
world history.

When Franklin Delano Roosevelt took office in March
1933, American and international politics and economics
were in a state of flux bordering on panic. The Gross National
Product of the United States was barely half its 1929 level,
and private investment had dropped more than 90 percent.

Net income of farmers was just one-fifth of what it had been in 1929, 13 million workers were unemployed, and the country's banking system was virtually insolvent. Overseas, world trade was nearly at a standstill and most debtor nations were in default. The United Kingdom, the great bastion of financial and commercial orthodoxy, had gone off the gold standard and moved to protect trade relations within the British Empire. Economic collapse was breeding political and military upheaval: Hitler was in power in Germany; most of Eastern Europe was moving toward similar dictatorships; and Japan's militarists had taken over the government, occupied Manchuria, and begun to move toward China proper.

The financial internationalists, whether they were Wilsonian Democrats or moderate Republicans, believed that the depth of the economic and political crises made it clearer than ever that the United States needed to lead the world toward an American version of the nineteenth-century *pax Britannica*. They stood for freer trade, and concurred with Winthrop Aldrich, chairman of the Chase National Bank, that, "the reduction of tariffs and the elimination of other impediments to the free interchange of goods among the nations . . . must be vigorously pressed if we are really to avoid the dangers of war."[2] The internationalists also wanted the United States to initiate financial and monetary cooperation among the Western powers in order to provide a stable international investment climate. Southern Democrats were the staunchest allies of the international bankers, for their traditional ties to export agriculture made them firm believers in international economic cooperation. The most highly placed spokesperson for the economic internationalists was Cordell Hull of Tennessee, Roosevelt's secretary of state, a fanatical free trader who fervently believed that, as he put it in 1937, "trade between nations is the greatest peacemaker and civilizer within human experience."[3]

Franklin Roosevelt himself had an internationalist pedigree, including service in the Wilson administration and his 1920 candidacy for the vice-presidency on a pro-League of Nations platform. Yet in 1933 the seriousness of the economic and political crises drove Roosevelt to turn his attention toward domestic recovery first, even at the expense of international economic cooperation. "Our international trade relations," Roosevelt said in his inaugural address, "are in point of time and necessity secondary to the establishment of a sound national economy."[4] In pursuit of this goal, the administration pushed through Congress a rapid-fire succession of bills—the National Recovery Act, the Agricultural Adjustment Act, the Tennessee Valley Development Act—to manage economic renewal.

The administration also enacted a series of major banking reforms. The most important was the Glass-Steagall Act of 1933, which separated commercial and investment banking. Congressional investigations had uncovered a number of instances from the 1920s in which bankers had used trust funds or consumer deposits they were managing to buy inferior bonds the bankers were trying to unload. There was clearly a risk that unscrupulous bankers could take advantage of their position as agents for both borrowers and lenders, both bond issuers and prospective bond purchasers. The solution was to prohibit investment banks from taking deposits, and to prohibit commercial banks from dealing in corporate securities. This effectively ended the days of organically linked financial and industrial combines, and by the time J. P. Morgan, Jr., died in 1943, the House of Morgan had been split into two independent financial institutions: the investment bank of Morgan Stanley and the commercial bank of the Morgan Guaranty Trust Company of New York. The overwhelming influence of the House of Morgan over

American financial markets was replaced by a more impersonal and institutionalized banking system.

International bankers were more interested in Roosevelt's
overseas initiatives than in his domestic policies. In one of his
first decisions, the president suspended the dollar's convertibility into gold, thus destroying what was left of the international gold standard. The bankers recognized that the international emergency forced the measure, and were reassured
by Roosevelt's May 1933 commitment to such goals as "a
cutting down of trade barriers" and "the setting up of a
stabilization of currencies."[5]

Roosevelt's economic internationalism, however, soon
gave way to his worries over the domestic economy. In July
1933, he lashed out at "old fetishes of so-called international
bankers" and broke up the London Economic Conference,
an important attempt at international economic cooperation.[6] James Warburg, an influential American banker, resigned in disgust as adviser to the State Department, and
Wall Street as a whole was shocked. A few months later, in
October, Roosevelt began intervening in the gold market to
devalue the dollar, a measure aimed at raising American
farm prices. The managed dollar devaluation violated the
sound-money principles of the international financial community, and Acting Treasury Secretary Dean Acheson, a
prominent Wall Street lawyer, handed in his resignation.

The early New Deal even made some concessions to leading economic nationalists. Roosevelt appointed one of them,
Hugh Johnson, head of the National Recovery Administration, and another, George Peek, head of the Agricultural
Adjustment Administration. Peek and Johnson represented
midwestern agricultural protectionism—Peek was an Illinois
farm equipment manufacturer; Johnson was a close business
and political associate of Peek's—and rejected any hint of

economic internationalism. In early 1934, Roosevelt put Peek in charge of the new export-import banks, and made him a special adviser to the president on foreign trade. The ascendancy of militant protectionists was a major blow to economic internationalists in the administration and on Wall Street, but it was not long before the policy pendulum swung back.

By 1935, the Roosevelt administration was edging toward economic internationalism. The charge on this front was led by Secretary of State Cordell Hull, who in June 1934 got Congress to pass the Reciprocal Trade Agreements Act, which allowed the president to negotiate lower tariffs without Congressional approval. The United States began moving toward freer trade, and within five years 60 percent of American imports entered under the new reciprocal agreements. In October 1934, Hugh Johnson resigned as head of the National Recovery Administration, and a few months later the Supreme Court declared it unconstitutional; in November 1935, George Peek, too, was forced out of the administration. Meanwhile the gold value of the dollar was stabilized at $35 an ounce, and Roosevelt began to encourage financial cooperation with the British and French. These efforts led to a three-way currency agreement late in 1936, which Belgium, the Netherlands, and Switzerland later joined.

Roosevelt transformed the American political system and America's overseas role in the 1930s, charting a careful course between orthodox internationalism and New Deal reform. During the late 1930s, as the economic emergency became less immediate and the international situation grew more worrisome, the Roosevelt administration's desire for international economic cooperation increased. On the eve of World War II there could be no doubt that the Roosevelt administration would be a hospitable place for those concerned with international economic and financial reconstruction.

As war began in Europe, Wall Street's economic internationalists flooded into the administration to plan for the postwar economic settlement. Some of the country's most prominent wartime and postwar figures came to government from the financial community. W. Averell Harriman—son of financier and railroad man E. H. Harriman and senior partner in the firm of Brown Brothers, Harriman—was perhaps America's best-known international envoy from 1941 to 1953. Harriman served successively as coordinator of Lend-Lease assistance to Britain, ambassador to the Soviet Union, ambassador to Great Britain, secretary of commerce, American overseer of the Marshall Plan, chief foreign affairs adviser to the president, and director of mutual security. Robert Lovett was a long-time associate of Harriman's, both in railroads and at the firm of Brown Brothers, Harriman; he started as assistant secretary of war for air, then became under secretary of state to George Marshall, then Marshall's deputy secretary of defense, and finally secretary of defense in his own right. James Forrestal, a close friend of Lovett's, left the presidency of the investment bank of Dillon, Read to serve as under secretary of the navy, then secretary of the navy, then secretary of defense until mental illness drove him from office and to suicide.

A number of Wall Street lawyers also served prominently. Dean Acheson came back to the administration in 1941, and progressed from assistant secretary to under secretary to secretary of state. John Foster Dulles, a Republican, was an important adviser to the Democratic administrations and then succeeded Acheson as secretary of state when Eisen-

hower took office. John McCloy was assistant secretary of
war, then president of the World Bank, then American high
commissioner in Germany. These veterans of the American
international financial establishment, and others less well
known, spent most of their time and energy between 1939
and 1955 in or around the government, helping to design
the postwar world.

The internationalists, both those who went to Washington
and those who remained in the private sector, wanted a
reconstructed world to be based on free trade, sound currencies, and international economic cooperation under American leadership. The United States would have to discard
once and for all the foreign-policy ambivalence international
bankers had confronted in the frustrating 1920s. As John
Foster Dulles said in 1942, "The old politico-economic order
has failed, and all the king's horses and all the king's men
cannot put it together again."[7] Free trade and capital movements were essential to the requisite new economic order.
Capital and goods could only flow freely across borders if the
currency wars of the 1930s were ended and a new international monetary system was built. The U.S.-British-French
stabilization agreement of 1936 was a good start; stabilization had to be extended after the war. Some favored a simple
return to the gold standard; others believed that monetary
stability might require abandoning strict gold-standard orthodoxy and relying more on intergovernmental cooperation under American guidance.

As Europe went to war, Dean Acheson summarized the
internationalist view in a well-known lecture at Yale in November 1939. Acheson pointed out the need for a new international order: "The economic and political system of the
Nineteenth Century has been for many years in the obvious
process of decline. The system is deeply impaired." Its pillars, Acheson said, were gone: "We can see that the credits

which were once extended by the financial center of London no longer provide the means for the production of wealth in other countries. We can see that the free trade areas, which once furnished both a market of vast importance and a commodities exchange, no longer exist. We can see that British naval power no longer can guarantee security of life and investment in distant parts of the earth."

Only purposive action by the United States government, Acheson argued, could reverse the disintegration of the world order. Certain measures were essential: "We can, for instance, join with other financially strong nations in making available capital in those parts of Europe which need productive equipment upon condition that Europe does its part to remove obstructions to trade within itself and provide, so far as it can, scope for commerce. We can join in offering a broader market for goods made under decent standards and, in this way, a means of purchasing essential raw materials. We can join in providing a stable international monetary system under which credits can be made and repaid and goods purchased and sold. We can join in removing exclusive or preferential trade arrangements with other areas created by military or financial conquest, agreement, or political connection."[8]

The economic internationalists were not alone in the Roosevelt administration in pressing for vigorous government leadership in the postwar world. Many New Deal reformers drew from the Depression the lesson that private markets could produce appalling results if left to themselves, and that government management of both domestic and international economic relations was essential. The New Dealers' postwar planning was led by Treasury Secretary Henry Morgenthau and by the Treasury's Harry Dexter White, who began work on the postwar economic order six months before the United States entered the war. Morgenthau and White fundamentally agreed with John Maynard Keynes, Great Britain's principal wartime international economic negotiator, regarding the Great Depression. In 1933, Keynes had written that "decadent but individualistic capitalism . . . is not a success. It is not intelligent, it is not beautiful, it is not just, it is not virtuous—and it doesn't deliver the goods."[9]

Like Keynes, the New Dealers regarded bankers with suspicion and favored national over international economic management. Morgenthau's relations with Wall Street were uneasy, and he later boasted, somewhat prematurely, that he and Roosevelt "moved the money capital from London and Wall Street to Washington, and they [the big bankers] hated us for it, and I'm proud of it."[10] For his part, Keynes believed that uncontrolled international financial flows could impede the kind of government economic intervention he felt was necessary to stabilize national economies; he had written in 1933, "above all, let finance be primarily national."[11]

American international bankers, although not unsympathetic to attempts to organize and rationalize markets, could hardly concur with the New Dealers' proposals to control private investment. During and after the war the concepts of the New Dealers and the economic internationalists clashed. After the Republicans swept Congress in 1946, even the traditional nationalists had to be reckoned with. The bankers were nonetheless able to bargain their way to an outcome they found acceptable.

In July 1944, at a resort in Bretton Woods, New Hampshire, negotiators from the United States, Great Britain, and the other Allied powers reached agreement on an International Monetary Fund and on an International Bank for Reconstruction and Development (World Bank). By December 1945, the requisite number of governments had signed the accords, and the International Monetary Fund and the World Bank opened their doors. The fundamental institutions of the new economic order were in place. The Bretton Woods system evolved under American leadership as a means to supervise the liberalization of international trade, finance, and investment. The system tied international goods and capital markets together as never before. Its start, however, was halting and contentious.

Harry Dexter White of Morgenthau's Treasury Department and John Maynard Keynes of the British Treasury designed much of the original Bretton Woods plan. These two principal architects of the Bretton Woods accords shared a general distaste for private international finance. Bankers in turn abhorred the unorthodox notions about deficit spending held by Keynes and the New Deal Treasury. As far as the Bretton Woods proposals were concerned, the principal disagreements centered on the proposed International Monetary Fund. Both groups, however, supported plans for trade liberalization and for the World Bank.

Most of the relevant activity on trade relations took place on unilateral American initiatives, since for the first time in many years American policymakers agreed on the need for trade liberalization. The principal target was Great Britain's system of trade preferences for its empire and dominions. Relentless pressure from the United States eventually broke the back of the Imperial Preference System, and opened the way for gradual trade liberalization.

The American attack on British trade policy began at the same time as did cooperation against the Nazis. The Atlantic Charter that Roosevelt and Churchill signed in August 1941 in effect committed the United States to enter the war in return for a clear statement of joint war aims. Freer trade was prominent among those aims. The two powers promised "to further the enjoyment by all states, great or small, victor or vanquished, of access, on equal terms, to the trade and to the raw materials of the world." Under Secretary of State Sumner Welles was explicit: "The Atlantic declaration means that every nation has a right to expect that its legitimate trade will not be diverted and throttled by towering tariff preferences, discriminations or narrow bilateral practices."[12]

The United States continued to pressure Britain to relax its system of trade preferences during the war. The Lend-Lease Agreement with Great Britain contained a series of economic principles, including a commitment to "the elimination of all forms of discriminatory treatment in international commerce, and to the reduction of tariff and other trade barriers."[13] A major postwar loan to Britain had as one of its purposes to, in the words of the agreement, "assist the Government of the United Kingdom to assume the obligations of multilateral trade." Winthrop Aldrich was more direct: "The British Commonwealth should agree to do away with exchange controls on current account and give up the so-called sterling area . . . relinquish the system of imperial preference and . . . eliminate quantitative trade controls."[14]

British trade liberalization was originally to be carried out under the auspices of a new International Trade Organization designed at Bretton Woods. Yet the new organization was aborted because of opposition within the United States. Protectionists thought it was too liberal, free traders thought it was too restrictive. It mattered little, in any event; trade liberalization proceeded apace under the improvised General Agreement on Tariffs and Trade (GATT). In four successive rounds of GATT negotiations from 1947 to 1956 the industrialized countries, led by the United States, moved decisively away from protectionism and toward commercial liberalization. The cycle of economic nationalism had been broken in trade.

American international bankers were pleased by commercial liberalization, and they also liked the Bretton Woods proposals for a World Bank. Keynes, White, and Wall Street alike recognized that private capital could not or would not undertake some large-scale, long-term projects essential to a healthy world economy: canals, port facilities, and irrigation works were a few examples. One possible solution had been proposed as early as 1931 by prominent New York banker Shepard Morgan, a veteran of the Bank for International Settlements: "a collateral institution . . . capable of granting long-term credits on its own responsibility and at its own risk." The new bank would have "authority to issue bonds in its own name" on the world's capital markets, and then re-lend the funds to worthy projects.[15]

The International Bank for Reconstruction and Development, or World Bank, would, as in Morgan's early proposal, borrow from private investors and lend for needy undertakings. Because the bank would finance investments that private investors would not, the financiers saw the bank as a useful adjunct to private capital flows, and generally supported the World Bank proposals. Wall Street lawyer John McCloy was appointed president of the World Bank in its first year, with Chase Bank's vice-president Eugene Black his right-hand man and eventual successor. McCloy and Black applied strict financial principles to the bank's operations, established a reputation for financial toughness, and inspired private-sector faith in the bank's bonds. Its first developmental loan, to Chile in 1948, was conditioned on Chile's making payments on previously defaulted debts. The World Bank was, in the eyes of the international bankers, a success.

International monetary relations were decisive for Wall Street, for international finance depends on predictable currency values. The interwar monetary system had been unable to prevent currencies from gyrating wildly, going onto and off of gold and generally making the international environment most unstable. Sound international monetary relations required a yardstick against which the world's currencies could be measured, and American international bankers felt that a gold-backed dollar was the appropriate yardstick. In 1943, Winthrop Aldrich expressed a widespread hope that after the war "the dollar would constitute a sure anchorage for the currencies of other nations and would become a generally acceptable international medium of exchange. All international transactions, including those of a bilateral or multilateral character, including the exportation or importation of goods, including short- or long-term capital movements, could be cleared on the basis of a dollar freely redeemable in gold."[16]

The bankers were suspicious of the Keynes-White proposal for an international fund for monetary stabilization. Keynes and White wanted an arrangement that would allow international trade and payments to take place without binding the hands of national policymakers. Keynes, after all, represented Great Britain; as likely postwar borrowers, the British wanted agreements to prohibit IMF influence over British economic policies. It worried the bankers enormously that the fund might dispense resources to nations without imposing conditions to force borrowers to pursue such financially "reasonable" policies as balanced budgets. The fund might thus allow the continuation of capital and exchange controls and function as a conduit for dollars to flow from the gullible United States to the profligate Europeans. It seemed to many American bankers that the IMF would relax or even replace the discipline that the market should impose on borrowing countries.

For these reasons, most Wall Street bankers opposed the IMF proposal when it came up in Congress. Harry Carr of the First National Bank of Philadelphia branded the proposal an example of "the same idealistic, but totally impractical collectivism that has characterized so much of the New Deal thinking"; Aldrich attacked the plan for "currency manipulation" as a "mechanism for instability." New York bankers preferred an American commitment to maintain the gold value of the dollar, coupled with Anglo-American cooperation to stabilize the pound sterling. Aldrich insisted that "the dollar-pound rate, the most important of all exchange rates, should be stabilized first."[17] With the world's two key currencies stabilized, the free market could do much of the rest.

The bankers' disapproval of the IMF did not keep Congress from passing the Bretton Woods agreements, but Wall Street did not give up the battle. The fund's voting structure gave the United States, and no one else, a veto; after the IMF opened for business, the American financial community had enough clout to ensure that American influence would be used to remake the fund. In the ten years after its creation, the IMF, prodded by the United States, codified stringent guidelines for borrowers from the fund. In effect, the IMF did not circumvent the discipline of the financial market, but came to reinforce it as a guardian of financial integrity.

The Bretton Woods institutions grew too slowly, however, to solve Europe's enormous postwar economic problems. The social and economic damage was so severe that the new order had to be postponed. More immediate and drastic measures were needed to get Europe on its feet.

American economic planners believed that the most important first step toward European economic recovery was to restore normalcy to London's City, a world financial center for nearly two hundred years. Normal international finance needed the City of London's participation and thus the freeing of the pound sterling from government controls. A major stabilization loan would allow Britain to help revive international financial markets.

In December 1945, the British signed an agreement to borrow $5 billion, three-quarters from the United States and one-quarter from Canada, to speed British financial recovery. To avoid a repetition of the post-World War I war debts tangle, the United States cancelled virtually all British Lend-Lease and other wartime obligations. In return for the low-interest loan and debt cancellation, the British agreed to remove most wartime controls on goods and capital movements and to restore sterling convertibility by July 1947.

The postwar loan to Britain had to be approved by Congress, however, and it thus became the first test of American political receptiveness to financing European reconstruction. The loan was originally presented as purely an economic arrangement, which would allow Britain to help build the Anglo-American partnership for an open world economy. The initial administration explanation was straightforward: "No other country has the same crucial position in world trade as England. Because of the wide use of the pound sterling in world trade, the large proportion of the world's trade which is carried on by the countries of the British Empire and the extreme dependence of England upon imports, the financial and commercial practices of Britain are of utmost importance in determining what kind of world economy we shall have."[18]

When the Senate debate on the loan began in the spring of 1946, it immediately became clear that economic arguments were not enough, and the specter of American isolationism reappeared. The Left opposed propping up the British Empire, the Right refused to aid the new Labour government, and Jewish and Irish Americans were loath to bail out the oppressor of Palestine and Ireland. Even economically, $3.75 billion seemed an exorbitant price to pay for lower British tariffs. Senator Arthur Vandenberg, ranking Republican on the Foreign Relations Committee, saw little reason why he and his colleagues should support the loan.

Secretary of State James Byrnes changed tactics, for he knew that Vandenberg's wing of the Republican party was far more susceptible to security arguments about the Soviet threat than to economic arguments. Byrnes told Vandenberg that the administration wanted to confront the Soviets more effectively, but that approval of the loan was a prerequisite. "When the Senate hearings ended in April," according to Dean Acheson's biographer David S. McLellan, "the loan's chances for passage still remained glum, and in order to improve its prospects, Byrnes reassured Vandenberg that the United States intended to maintain its policy of firmness at the forthcoming Foreign Ministers Conference in Paris. Reassured, Vandenberg warned his colleagues (invoking the anti-Soviet bias for the first time): 'If we do not lead some other and powerful nation will capitalize on our failure and we shall pay the price of our default.' Acheson regarded it as unfortunate that the loan had to be justified with veiled illusions to the Soviet threat, but he accepted it as a price that had to be paid to secure the support needed."[19]

The Senate passed the agreement, and in the bitter House battle, the Soviet threat again became the decisive argument. Majority leader McCormack warned that failure to pass the loan would leave "those countries who look toward Washington with a friendly eye no alternative but to be subjected to the sphere of influence of Moscow." Minority leader Jessie Wolcott came around to support the loan, since it now appeared to determine "whether there shall be a coalition between the British sphere and the American sphere or whether there shall be a coalition between the British sphere and the Soviet sphere."[20]

Congress approved the British loan, but as it turned out,

the financial planners had underestimated the war's devastating effects. The British economy was still in shambles and business confidence was low. When sterling became convertible on July 15, 1947, capital rushed out of Britain. In a matter of weeks, British dollar reserves nearly disappeared, and much of the multibillion-dollar loan was dissipated. Exchange controls were clamped on, not to be removed for another ten years.

The British disaster demonstrated that enormous sums were needed to get the European economies running and participating again in the world economy. The logical place to turn was the International Bank for Reconstruction and Development—the World Bank. But the Bank had—as the bankers wanted—been set up to make good investments, and Europe in 1947 was hardly a good investment. Only massive injections of American money could revive the struggling European economies. Yet once more the planners faced the prospect of finding, as they did after World War I, that Americans were unwilling to spend taxpayers' money to mend Europe's wounds.

Domestic opposition to American financing of European reconstruction was indeed strong. The Taft Republicans and other neo-isolationists, who would just as soon have left Europe to its own devices, seemed on the rise, and the Republican party swept the House and Senate in 1946.

Congressional support for postwar aid was obtained by linking economic internationalism, unpopular with the Republicans, with anticommunism and national security, which they could hardly appear to ignore. American aid for the construction of an open world economy was presented as part of the fight against Soviet-led communism, and this made America's far-reaching postwar commitments palatable to the potential domestic opposition.

To be sure, economic internationalists like the bankers

were also concerned with the spread of communism. This was not just a problem in the areas of Central and Eastern Europe liberated by the Red Army or by Communist guerrillas. Especially in Italy, France, and Belgium, the old ruling classes faltered between discredited reaction and discouraged irresoluteness, while the Communists and their allies seemed capable of using peaceful electoral means to parlay their anti-Fascist credentials and broad working-class popularity into state power. As Acheson recalled the era, "only in Britain and Russia did people have any confidence in government, or social or economic organization, or currencies. Elsewhere governments had been repudiated, or abolished by the conquerors; social classes were in bitter enmity, with resistance groups hunting out and executing, after drumhead trials, collaborators with the late enemy."[21]

With Europe near starvation and the Communists powerful, the Continent might opt out of the *pax Americana*. Presidential aide Joseph Jones wrote to Senator William Benton, "If these areas are allowed to spiral downwards into economic anarchy, then at best they will drop out of the United States orbit and try an independent nationalist policy; at worst they will swing into the Russian orbit."[22] Indeed, James Forrestal told President Truman in March 1947 that the Soviets held out hope to the starving Europeans: "Russia has a product which is skillfully tailored to appeal to people who are in despair—and thanks to German and Japanese aggression, Russia has had a wealth of customers who are sufficiently desperate to turn to anything." For America to prevail it had to outbid the economic attractions of communism: "By providing outstanding economic leadership, this country can wage its attack successfully—and can thereby build the foundations of a peaceful world. For the only way in which a durable peace can be created is by world-wide restoration of economic activity and international trade."[23]

The economic internationalists saw their plans for economic reconstruction as an effective bulwark against the Left. Postwar policymakers went a step further, though, and redefined the enemy to include not just the political threat of social revolution but the military threat of Soviet aggression. There is little question that this redefinition was in large part an attempt to overcome the reticence of domestic political forces to finance European reconstruction. A pattern was established in which American support for European reconstruction and an open world economy was advocated on the grounds of opposing Soviet expansion.

By early 1947, as further evidence of the seriousness of the war's destruction accumulated, it was apparent that far more American aid was needed. "Communist movements," said Assistant Secretary of State Will Clayton, "are threatening established governments in every part of the globe. These movements, directed by Moscow, feed on economic and political weakness. . . . The only way to meet this challenge is by a vast new program of assistance given directly by the United States itself."[24] The program began with beleaguered Greece and Turkey.

Arthur Vandenberg, now chair of the Senate Foreign Relations Committee, was once again reluctant, as were many of his colleagues in the Republican-controlled Congress. In a major White House meeting with Congressional leaders, Secretary of State George Marshall asked for support, but most unconvincingly. Dean Acheson took over, painting the darkest of pictures: "Only two great powers remain in the world . . . the United States and the Soviet Union." The confrontation was fundamental, Acheson said, with "one great power being a democracy, laying its stress upon the worth of the individual . . . while the other great power is a police state exerting rigid control over the individual."

America had to decide between "acting with energy or losing by default." Acheson ended; the Congressional leaders were silent. Finally Senator Vandenberg told Truman: "Mr. President, if you will say that to the Congress and the country, I will support you and I believe that most of its members will do the same."[25]

The Truman Doctrine, with the assent of much of the Republican party's neo-isolationist wing, committed the United States to massive economic aid to its allies. A few months later the government unveiled the Marshall Plan. As the East-West divide in Europe hardened, the United States poured $15 billion over five years into strengthening the economic and social stability of its allies in the battle against the Soviet Union. The aid served both to revitalize Europe's struggling economies and to tie Western Europe together into a more cohesive economic and political unit.

The United States did not reconstruct Western Europe, however, simply by throwing money at it. The task was as political as it was economic; Western Europe's economies had to be revived and its political systems rebuilt to eliminate the legacy of economic nationalism. In this ambitious endeavor European economic integration, an old favorite of America's bankers in the 1920s, was resurrected.

To American postwar policymakers, the incessant attempts of Europe's small nations at economic self-sufficiency on a national basis seemed both absurd and inherently warlike. The best way to avoid another Continental war was to tie the Western European economies together in a web of economic interdependence. The ensuing prosperity would defuse a major cause of European national rivalries. The idea was hardly new: Dean Acheson had said in 1939 that aid to postwar Europe should be given "upon condition that Europe does its part to remove obstructions to trade within itself." In 1941, John Foster Dulles wrote that "the reestablishment of some twenty-five wholly independent sovereign states in Europe would be political folly," and that the United States should therefore "seek the political reorganization of Continental Europe as a federated commonwealth."[26]

As the Cold War developed and Europe became unalterably divided, Western European economic cooperation was urgent. The United States would not provide massive aid simply to intensify national economic antagonism among the capitalist nations of Western Europe, and accordingly it conditioned Marshall Plan aid on joint European coordination of its use.

Planning for a more lasting institutional framework for European economic integration began in 1950. In January, German Chancellor Konrad Adenauer proposed to John McCloy, who had left the presidency of the World Bank to become American high commissioner in Germany, that the coal and steel industries of the Ruhr and Saar regions be internationalized. French Planning Commissioner Jean Monnet rapidly picked up Adenauer's idea. Monnet had long experience in dealing with Americans, especially American bankers. He had been vice-president of Blair and Co., a New York investment bank, in the 1920s, and later of Transamerica, the owner of the Bank of America. With Blair, he had helped arrange American loans to Eastern Europe and worked closely with John Foster Dulles on such matters as the 1927 Polish stabilization and the liquidation of the Swedish-based Kruger-Toll conglomerate. In America, Monnet had also collaborated with John McCloy in 1940 and 1941, and he was a friend of Dean Acheson's. Monnet shared with the American financiers a profound belief in the harmfulness of economic nationalism, in the need for American leadership in the postwar world, and in the desirability of Western European economic unity. Monnet had long dreamed of "a true yielding of sovereignty by European nations to some kind of central union."[27] By 1950, with American support, the time was right.

Monnet quickly drew up a proposal to place the coal and steel industries of France and Germany under joint management as the first step to broader economic accord. On April 30, Foreign Minister Robert Schuman approved the plan; on May 7, Dean Acheson agreed to it; and on May 9, the French cabinet authorized the so-called Schuman Plan. The result was the European Coal and Steel Community, with Monnet as president; in 1957, following the blueprint of Monnet's Action Committee for the United States of Europe, the European Economic Community, or Common Market, joined the Coal and Steel Community. Western European economic integration had begun.

The journey begun at Versailles in 1919, left unfinished for so long, had ended. American international bankers had tried to get the American government to support European reconstruction and an open world economy after World War I and had failed. It had taken the Depression, World War II, and the Cold War to achieve what Thomas Lamont in 1947 called "the mighty goal that Woodrow Wilson visualized for mankind and that he had to leave to others."[28] The mighty goal was a reality, and after a twenty-year hiatus in which their exertions shifted from private finance to government policy, American international bankers could get back to business. What John Foster Dulles had said a few years after World War I was just as appropriate in the 1940s as it was in the 1920s: "The prosperity of this nation is dependent upon the economic and financial revival of Europe. . . . Our national policy, dictated by our national self-interest, calls for the economic rehabilitation of Europe. . . . Generally speaking, we want the rest of the world to grow rich—so that we may get some of its wealth."[29]

Although America's international bankers focused their attention on events overseas during the 1940s and early 1950s, some domestic issues deeply concerned them, especially government monetary policy. The needs of wartime government spending had, since the late 1930s, dominated monetary policy. The government borrowed massively to fund the war effort, and the Treasury Department, the government's borrowing agency, kept interest rates artificially low in order to make government borrowing as inexpensive as possible. The new burst of government spending after 1947—the Marshall Plan, rearmament, and the Korean War—strengthened the Treasury's resolve to hold interest rates down.

The bankers were willing to put up with restraints on interest rates so long as the war went on. When it was over, as postwar inflation ate away at bank profits, the financial community chafed at the Treasury Department's insistence on low interest rates for government borrowing. Treasury policy became unbearable as the Korean War fueled inflation. From 1941 to 1951, the interest rate on Treasury bills averaged 0.6 percent a year, while inflation was 6 percent a year, so that the bills actually had a negative interest rate of −5.4 percent a year. The bankers felt that negative real interest rates both depressed bank earnings and kept inflation high.

From 1948 on, the bankers pressed the Treasury to release interest rates and return primary responsibility for monetary policy to the Federal Reserve System. The Treasury, after all, had a vested interest in making government borrowing cheap, while the Fed was more responsive to the needs of the financial community. As Allan Sproul, president of the Federal Reserve Bank of New York, wrote to the head of the American Bankers' Association in early 1951, "there is going to have to be a determination . . . whether we are going to be able to have a credit policy somewhat divorced from the stark needs of Treasury borrowing. . . . The Treasury has demanded, in effect, that we give fixed support to the government securities market at present levels as part of what it calls financial mobilization for defense. That means the abandonment of all control over bank reserves, as was the case during the war, and it helps to expose the country to another round of dollar debasement such as we inherited from our war finance. I should think the banks of the country would want us to use all our powers to help prevent such a tragic encore."[30]

After years of bickering, the Federal Reserve regained power. In March 1951, the Treasury and the Fed announced an agreement known as the Treasury Accord that essentially returned independent control of monetary policy to the Fed after a decade of deviations. Federal Reserve monetary policy made inflation fighting a prime consideration, and interest rates on Treasury bills immediately rose from an annual average of 0.6 percent between 1941 and 1951 to an annual average of 2.6 percent from 1952 to 1967. As inflation plummeted from 6 to 1.5 percent a year, *real* interest rates (that is, allowing for inflation) went from −5.4 percent to +1.2 percent.[31] The central role of the Federal Reserve System— by definition, by constitution, and by preference a close ally of the private banking system—was affirmed.

By the late 1950s, reconstruction was over and the way was clear for a revival of private international finance. America's protectionist predilections had been reversed; its tariffs were at their lowest levels in over a century and were declin ing. The European colonial empires and their preferential economic arrangements were all but dismantled. The Common Market was finally reducing economic conflict in Western Europe. The International Bank for Reconstruction and Development, under the leadership of former Chase vice-president Eugene Black, was lending $700 million a year and the World Bank staff was teaching financial responsibility to fifty nations and territories. The International Monetary Fund was a reliable international financial police officer, dispensing both loans and performance requirements to increasing numbers of borrowers.

The agreement of the major nations of Western Europe to make their currencies convertible in the last week of 1958 symbolized the fact that the new world economy was definitely open for business. From that time on, the Western European currencies were more or less freely traded on currency markets, and their values were pegged to the dollar, which itself was pegged to gold at $35 an ounce since Roosevelt's successful attempt at stabilization. American bankers had long awaited the return to currency convertibility; as Michael Heilperin of *Fortune* magazine had written in 1953, "only when full convertibility has been won will the American investor be able to invest abroad in full assurance that the sole risks he has to face are the usual business risks and that he is free from arbitrary action by foreign governments . . . it is only then that the American productive system will be able to look upon the entire world as its market in full confidence that the 'merit system' prevails and that the principles of free markets and free enterprise are acknowledged and respected."[32]

With Europe's currencies freed, with the World Bank and the IMF trustworthy and active, and with trade liberalization and European integration progressing, America's international bankers faced a friendly world. Their balance sheets, and those of their customers, already reflected the success of the new economic order. American exports were nearly $20 billion a year, six or seven times their prewar level. American corporations increased their overseas investments from $8 billion in 1945 to $32 billion in 1960. By 1960, American banks had over $8 billion in foreign loans outstanding, their foreign lending was running at over a billion dollars a year, and American bond markets were lending another $600 million a year to foreigners. Overseas branch networks were growing rapidly, and by 1965, Citibank—the market leader—had 163 offices and affiliates in fifty-five nations, nearly triple the 1955 figure.[33] As Walter Page of Morgan Guaranty told *Fortune* magazine, "It is the foreign facilities that have the sex appeal in this banking game."[34]

In 1961, as international finance began to grow for the first time in thirty years, David Rockefeller of the Chase Manhattan Bank told Congress: "I believe the United States must exercise a role of leadership in international financial matters. This is a part—an important part—of our role in contributing to the defense and development of the free world." The New York banks were financing world trade, lending to foreigners, and attracting foreign-owned dollar deposits. "All of these matters," Rockefeller told Congress, "not only have important economic implications for the United States but also add to the political strength and position of leadership of the United States in world affairs. Today New York City in many ways is the financial center of the world. That is an inevitable accompaniment of the nation's position in political and military affairs. We cannot have one without the other."[35]

In the early 1960s, however, international finance took an

unprecedented turn toward what came to be known as the offshore markets, or Euromarkets. Soon hundreds of billions of dollars were flowing untrammeled across borders with a speed and fluidity that even America's most optimistic international bankers could not have imagined in the 1930s and 1940s. On the basis of the postwar world economy that American planners designed, international bankers brought together the largest and most mobile pool of capital in world history.

4

The Euromarkets

Today's international financial markets constitute a pool of capital of almost unimaginable size. The offshore markets in which most international banking takes place hold almost $3 trillion. If one subtracts transactions among banks themselves, the market's net size is well over a trillion dollars. Even the lower figure is staggering: it is equal to the entire output of China's 1 billion people in four years. The market's trillion dollars could buy every manufacturing corporation in the United States, as well as the livestock, crops, buildings, and machinery on all of America's farms.

This huge pool of capital is not stagnant. In an average year, banks and other investors in the offshore markets lend $300 billion to governments and nonfinancial corporations. Since the early 1970s, about half the borrowers have been from North America, Western Europe, and Japan; a third are from the non-OPEC developing countries; and the rest are about evenly split between OPEC and Communist borrowers. The approximately $300 billion that international financial markets lend out every year is roughly equal to what America's corporations borrow in three normal years, or what they invest in a normal year. In other words, every year international banks lend enough to purchase every new factory, railroad, port, ship, power plant, and other productive facility built in America in that year, along with all the new machinery inside them; or to buy all of the new private homes and apartment houses built in the United States during three average years.

Banks all over the world are tied electronically to these enormous international financial markets. They can shift millions of dollars around the globe, or trade billions of yen for Deutsche marks, in a matter of minutes. They can put together billion dollar loans for major governments and multinational corporations in a few days. Their ability to respond instantaneously to economic and political events has transformed the world economy.

The extraordinary integration of international financial markets has major implications for domestic economic and political relations within the world's nations, including the United States. International financial flows challenge the economic interests of those disfavored by international investors; they circumvent the authority of national political leaders. Modern American international finance now threatens to call forth the sort of domestic opposition faced by its predecessor in the 1920s. The international banking system is in fact eroding the international and domestic, economic and political underpinnings of the postwar world order.

Today's international financial system is a unique global network known as the offshore markets, or Euromarkets. The Euromarkets arose in the 1950s and came to dominate international finance in the 1960s. They were in large part a result of attempts by American bankers and politicians to avoid the domestic political furor that American foreign lending caused before World War II. As American international banking began to clash with domestic economic goals, policymakers attempted to postpone the conflict by allowing financial institutions to squeeze through cracks in national regulations. The ultimate result was to accelerate the expansion of a free-wheeling international financial system of unprecedented size.

Ironically, the Eurodollar market, the ultimate in capitalist internationalism, originally grew out of the financial needs of the Soviet Union and China. In the late 1940s and early 1950s, at the height of the Cold War, the Soviet and Chinese governments dared not deposit in banks in the United States dollars earned through overseas trade, for fear that the American government would seize the Communist millions. Because the capitalist world was starved for dollars, it was not hard for the Soviets and Chinese to find banks in London, including some Soviet-owned trade banks, that were happy to hold dollars and eventually to lend them.

Soon London's bankers invented a new international financial concept: Eurocurrency, or offshore currency deposits, defined as currency held outside its country of issue—for example, dollars in London or Swiss francs in Luxembourg. Regulatory responsibility was confused from the start, since there was little precedent for a country to control the use of its currency outside its borders. To take the most common case, Eurodollars in London, the American government could hardly claim authority over banks in Great Britain, even if they were using dollars, while British authorities had no reason to regulate the use of another country's currency so long as the transactions did not leak directly into the British economy. Matters were complicated by the large number of foreign banks in London, so that the relevant question might be, Who was going to supervise dollar deposits in a German bank's branches on British soil? The answer came quickly enough: nobody.

By the early 1960s, London was doing a tidy business in offshore dollars, or Eurodollars. The market was very short term, and deposits and loans were made for at most a few months. Nonetheless, high Euromarket interest rates attracted depositors. American corporations with subsidiaries in Europe, wealthy European investors, and many foreign governments used Eurodollar deposits to earn a better return on their dollars than they could in the United States. In 1964, Paul Einzig, a long-time observer of the London financial scene, also detected an interesting new set of Eurodollar deposits with "the growing popularity of that form of investment among Arabian recipients of oil royalties. The rulers of various oil-producing territories in the Middle East appear to have acquired a taste for investing a large part of their receipts in Euro-dollars and Euro-sterling."[1] The offshore markets had attracted so much interest on the part of depositors, borrowers, and bankers that when American international banking was pushed out of Wall Street by a U.S. government afraid of its domestic consequences, it moved easily to the Euromarkets.

In the early 1960s, as American lending to foreigners grew rapidly, it began to collide with the domestic and international imperatives of the new American empire. The United States paid for its global military and diplomatic commitments with dollars, and the country's ability to do so depended on the willingness of foreigners to accept dollars in payment. In the dollar-thirsty world of 1953, this was not a problem, but burgeoning military expenditures in Europe and Southeast Asia flooded the world with dollars in the 1960s, and the "dollar gap" of the 1950s became a "dollar glut."

The United States was spending more dollars abroad than foreigners were willing to accept, and as dollars became more common, pressure built for the dollar's value to fall. Yet devaluing the dollar meant abandoning America's premier position in international monetary affairs, in which the dollar was "as good as gold." Foreign lending from the

United States simply exacerbated the problem by providing more dollars to foreigners. Continued overseas lending from the United States would have required either that the country give up some of its costly military commitments in Europe or Southeast Asia or that it sacrifice its unique international monetary position. Neither road appealed to the Kennedy and Johnson administrations.

An alternative to scaling back U.S. government spending overseas was to cut down on purchases of foreign goods by Americans and to increase sales of American goods on foreign markets; this would have brought some of the excess dollars back to the United States. If American exports increased and imports declined, fewer dollars would be sent abroad as payment for foreign goods and more would come into the United States as foreigners bought more American goods. The standard formula for expanding exports, though, is to cut wages, while the way to reduce imports is to cut consumption. Again, neither choice was attractive to the American authorities.

The revitalization of American international banking threatened to undermine the political agreements that had made it possible. Domestic political opposition to international economic integration after World War II had been defused in two ways: first, economic internationalism was presented as crucial to national security; second, economic internationalism was presented as essential to domestic prosperity. In the early 1960s, international financial integration began to come into conflict with both national security and domestic prosperity.

The nation faced increasingly serious pressure on the balance of payments. If the dollar outflow continued, the central role of U.S. currency in the world economy would be in danger. To reduce the dollar drain, Americans had either to spend less abroad and curtail American globalism, or spend less at home and reduce domestic prosperity. Every dollar foreigners borrowed from New York banks and bond markets increased the international surplus of dollars and made the bind more constricting.

In 1963, Americans lent over $2 billion to foreigners. The Kennedy administration, forced to act, moved to restrict the outflow of dollars from Wall Street. The government imposed a tax on most foreign bonds issued in the United States, and soon afterward strictly limited the amount that banks in the United States could lend to foreigners and that American corporations could send abroad to invest. The idea was to slow the outflow of capital from the United States, so that neither overseas government spending nor domestic consumption would have to be reduced.

This system of capital controls lasted until 1974, but it did not stop American banks and corporations from lending and investing overseas. Indeed, it speeded the internationalization of American finance, by pushing American banks onto the unregulated Euromarkets. Instead of drawing dollars out of the United States, the international banks and corporations used the rapidly growing Euromarkets to get dollars already offshore for their loans and investments. American banks strengthened their branches in London, for example, to attract dollar deposits and lend them there. American multinationals invested abroad with money they borrowed abroad, instead of with American capital.

Offshore dollar lending exploded as a response to restrictions on foreign lending from New York. In the words of the Chase Manhattan Bank's Eugene Birnbaum, "the market for international dollar financing shifted from New York to Europe. Foreign dollar loans that had previously come under the regulatory guidelines or examination of U.S. government agencies simply moved out of their jurisdictional reach. The result has been the amassing of an immense volume of liquid funds and markets—the world of Eurodollar finance—outside the regulatory authority of *any* country or agency."[2]

As American banks and corporations went on expanding overseas even with capital controls, an unregulated, offshore alternative to Wall Street sprang up. By 1970, the Euromarkets' net size (that is, subtracting transactions among banks themselves) was $65 billion, and three years later it reached $160 billion. For every dollar that American banks lent from American soil, they were lending six or seven more from the offshore markets. In the early 1970s, the offshore banks and bondholders lent $35 billion a year. The world's international bankers were lending more in two years than they had in the previous century. "The banking business," remarked Robert Lutz of Credit Suisse, "is now going through one of the most rapid periods of change in its long history."[3]

The Euromarkets had an extraordinary ability to attract money and move it from place to place. In 1970, Chase's William Butler noted approvingly that "the growing volume of international financial transactions has been handled with greater efficiency and dispatch than would have been possible under any other conceivable arrangement."[4] Every major international corporation came to the offshore markets to deposit money and look for loans. Big investors, including the increasingly wealthy Arab oil magnates, deposited more and more into the markets, attracted by high interest rates and by what Citibank's Julien-Pierre Koszul in 1970 called "a marvelous platform from which it is easy to rebound, in any direction, to any country, into any currency—and with anonymity."[5]

Even as Koszul wrote, this "marvelous platform" was helping to undermine the Bretton Woods monetary system. The problem was deeper than the Euromarkets; the underlying difficulty was in adapting to a world economy in which the

United States, and the dollar, were no longer uniquely powerful. By 1958, the Western Europeans and Japanese had rebuilt, and their currencies were strong. Western Europe and Japan went from economic strength to strength; between 1950 and 1973, the French, German, and Italian economies grew twice as fast as that of the United States on a per-person basis, while Japan's economy grew nearly four times as rapidly.

Rapid growth in the Western European and Japanese economies made those countries strong competitors of the United States in wealth and dynamism, and over the course of the 1960s, the U.S. dollar gradually lost perceived value to European currencies. Under the Bretton Woods system, the U.S. government could not devalue the dollar—it was "as good as gold"—but as firms and individuals around the world got rid of the dollars they no longer trusted, the only way governments could maintain the U.S. currency's official price was to buy up dollars, a proposition that soon became prohibitively expensive. As the world economy became less unilateral, the gold-dollar system began to disintegrate.

The underlying imbalance in international monetary relations was complicated by the ability of banks in the free-wheeling Euromarkets to shift into and out of currencies and markets in a matter of minutes. When world trade and finance were at a relatively low level, governments could easily intervene in foreign exchange markets to keep currency values stable, but the extraordinary expansion of international capital flows by the 1960s made it hard to hold currencies firmly in line. With international banks, corporations, and private investors dealing in billions of dollars a day, national governments found it too expensive to protect their currencies from speculative attack. As enormous financial flows buffeted the dollar, Citibank's Koszul warned in 1970 that the international banking system's efficiency in raising and moving funds had a darker side: "The same funds which accumulate in larger and larger quantities on the Eurodollar market to evade real or imaginary perils stand ready to run toward countries or currencies which seem to offer opportunities for earning, safety or exchange profit. In short, the Eurodollar market enjoys an expanding base, but a more and more volatile one."[6]

The Bretton Woods system collapsed for related domestic and international reasons. Internationally, as Western Europe and Japan rebuilt, and international trade and finance grew, international monetary relations could not keep pace. The United States found it increasingly difficult to manage a dollar-based international system, especially with the increasing importance of other economic powers and with the destabilizing influence of the offshore financial markets. Domestically, within the United States opposition to economic integration was growing rapidly. Foreign competition was intense, and it was exacerbated by a dollar that was artificially expensive compared to other currencies. Domestic political pressure for protection from imports surged, fed by an overvalued dollar that could not last. Pressure on the dollar eventually forced Richard Nixon to devalue it in 1971; over the next few years the Bretton Woods system gradually disintegrated.

By 1975, the dollar was no longer backed by gold and the world's major currencies were left to fluctuate more or less freely on international currency markets. The international monetary system designed at Bretton Woods gave way to a market-based order in which dollars, Deutsche marks, and yen bring only what investors, bankers, and traders are willing to pay. Governments sometimes step in to stop a steep rise or decline in their currency's price, but in general, international monetary relations are now a modified free-for-all.

Although the major Western economic powers revised the

international monetary system in the 1970s, they continued to encourage free capital movements. If anything, the move from the gold-dollar standard to floating exchange rates reinforced the position of financial markets in the world economy, because foreign-currency traders, rather than governments, came to determine currency values. As international lending and investment grew even more rapidly after 1971 than before, the new environment gave ever greater room for the Euromarkets to influence the world political economy.

The offshore financial markets amply demonstrated their extraordinary efficiency in raising and moving funds in 1974, when they absorbed about $30 billion in deposits from the members of the Organization of Petroleum Exporting Countries (OPEC), and lent out some $60 billion in the midst of the most serious economic crisis in forty years. When OPEC quadrupled petroleum prices in December 1973, such countries as Saudi Arabia and Kuwait suddenly had tens of billions of dollars that they could not immediately and reasonably spend on their tiny populations. Between a third and a half of OPEC's excess billions went to the Euromarkets, a total of $150 billion between 1974 and 1980. The international banks generally found lucrative uses for the funds deposited with them, especially among a few rapidly industrializing nations in Latin America, Asia, and Africa. In the 1970s, the less developed countries borrowed $200 billion on the offshore markets.

The offshore financial markets now hold over $2 trillion in deposits. The world's largest banks move tens of billions of dollars every day to and from Singapore, London, Bahrain, Luxembourg, the Bahamas, and dozens of other financial centers. The markets are so powerful, and so important to the world's major capitalist economies, that many governments now permit offshore financial operations, exempt from most national regulations, to take place on their soil. Since 1981, banks have been able to set up International Banking Facilities in the United States to operate in the global offshore markets exempt from U.S. domestic regulation. Offshore financial markets have become a central feature of the modern international economy.

There is, of course, historical precedent for banks from the world's wealthy nations to have major foreign interests. Dutch, British, French, and German banks have centuries of international financial experience. Foreign lending may have been as important for the U.S. financial system between World War I and the Depression as are its current overseas ties. American banks and bondholders are now owed about $500 billion by foreigners, as against about $11 billion in 1929. In the interim, of course, inflation and economic growth have changed the meaning of such figures, and in fact, in both cases the amount owed was equal to about 11 or 12 percent of the country's Gross National Product. In a sense, America's international bankers have simply picked up where they left off when interrupted by the Depression and World War II.

Although there is nothing new about banks from the United States and other nations lending to foreigners, a very great deal about today's international financial markets is unprecedented. Before the Euromarkets, international finance was safely ensconced *within* existing national financial markets. When the state of Alabama or the province of Buenos Aires wanted to borrow money in London in the nineteenth century, they simply approached a British "merchant bank"—an investment bank in American jargon—to manage the details. The merchant bank arranged for the bonds to be issued and sold to British investors, took a percentage of the proceeds as a commission, and handed the remaining pounds sterling over to Alabama or Buenos Aires for whatever uses they had in mind. Private American or Argentine firms might borrow directly from British banks for short periods of time to finance imports or exports.

Foreign lending in the pre-Euromarket age was very much a part of national economies. British investors bought "Argentine 6s," Argentine bonds paying 6 percent interest, much as they bought bonds of the London subway system. Once New York became an international financial center, American investors on Wall Street similarly bought and sold the bonds of Germany, Peru, or Poland just as they bought stocks or bonds of General Motors, and probably bought them from the same investment banks and brokers. A few big American commercial banks extended foreign trade credits to American and foreign corporations from the New York money market. Foreign borrowers in London or New York joined domestic corporations and local governments in tapping stock, bond, and money markets.

Today the Euromarkets tie the world's investors, borrowers, and banks together in a network that is at the same time part of no national financial system and part of them all. When Buenos Aires or Alabama borrow abroad now, they are as likely to borrow Deutsche marks in Singapore or dollars in Luxembourg as they are to borrow pounds in London or dollars on Wall Street; even the U.S. government has taken to borrowing dollars in Europe and Japan. The world's major banks have come together from dozens of countries in a denationalized zone of financial neutrality. This banking Twilight Zone belongs to no nation, is governed by no country's laws, and is subject to little or no regulation.

The central ingredient of this monetary no-man's-land is relaxed regulation and supervision by national authorities. Offshore markets are also exempt from many of the legal requirements of national financial markets. Deposits in

American banks offshore, for example, are not insured by the Federal Deposit Insurance Corporation (FDIC), and banks are required to hold only 3 percent of their deposits in reserve as against three or four times that proportion in the United States. On the Euromarkets, unlike at home, American banks can deal in commercial and investment banking, both taking deposits and selling bonds. There is no Euromarket ban on bank branching, no troublesome state legislature to scrutinize community loans, no Congress to prohibit interstate banking, no public opinion to complain of redlining and long lines.

Eurobankers deal primarily with other Eurobankers; over half of all offshore business is between banks. Most of the rest is with major multinational corporations, big institutional investors, and governments. This is a market for the "heavy hitters" seeking to borrow, trade currencies, and make deposits in multiples of a million dollars. Loans in the billions of dollars are not rare.

The offshore markets are indeed attractive to large depositors and borrowers. The relative insulation of these markets from the whims of national authorities makes them appealing to governments that might be subject to financial intervention for political purposes, as well as to large private investors interested in evading taxes. The fact that banks doing business on the offshore markets are generally free from national financial regulations, and that international banks deal only with very large deposits or loans, allows the offshore markets to pay more to depositors, charge less to borrowers, and use the very latest in telecommunications technology and financial innovations. The combination of state-of-the-art technology and relative freedom from government interference makes the offshore markets the financial marketplace of choice for the world's leading banks and corporations.

This great international financial system is important, both for its size and because it forms the apex of a pyramid whose base is the national economies of the entire capitalist world. The huge financial institutions that dominate the offshore markets in turn hold sway over the financial markets of their home nation. The United States is a good example. Nine American commercial banks—Citibank, Chase, Morgan Guaranty, Manufacturers Hanover, Bankers Trust, and Chemical, all of New York; Bank of America and Security Pacific of California; and First Chicago—account for the vast majority of American international financial activities. They are joined abroad by five leading investment banks—First Boston, Morgan Stanley, Salomon Brothers, Merrill Lynch, and Goldman Sachs. These few internationally prominent banks from the United States largely determine the contours and direction of the entire American financial market. The five investment banks do two-thirds of all bond underwriting in the United States. The leading commercial banks have about one-third of the resources of the entire American banking system among them, and each of them is several hundred times the size of the average American bank. When Chase or Citibank lowers or raises its prime lending rate, other banks follow suit.

Around the world, the largest banks from every major non-Communist nation have become international, and with several dozen counterparts from other countries, they lead the international banking system. All nations are drawn into the international financial whirlwind: Their economies depend on their domestic financial system, the financial systems are led by a few big banks, and these few banks are part of the tightly knit world of international finance.

The offshore financial markets contain more capital than has ever been brought together in all of world history, and they are a major force in the economies of all of the world's nations. No corporation, investor, or government is insulated from trends in international banking. Investment, production, and commerce all rely on the banks; international currency movements, international trade, and international investment flow through the banks; governments plan and execute their policies with a close eye on the international financial reaction.

The offshore markets have both long- and short-term components. Their most important long-term activity is lending, either as bank credits or as Eurobonds. The markets are able to make enormous loans of great importance at a moment's notice, and we shall have more to say about this soon. The short end of the market includes very short-term deposits and loans, often for only a night, and especially trading in currencies. With the assistance of modern telecommunications, these day-to-day Euromarket activities link money markets around the world.

The Euromarkets, first and foremost, provide a market for foreign currencies. They are in fact often known as Eurocurrency markets, and in their early days they were primarily used by governments and corporations to buy, sell, or hold foreign currencies in reserve. Corporations that trade or invest overseas, and governments of nations whose corporations trade and invest overseas, need a ready source of supply and demand for the currencies they are using or earning. Because the Euromarkets are not part of any national banking system, on the Euromarkets *all* currencies are foreign currencies, and the Euromarkets trade currencies faster, more cheaply, and in larger quantities than they have ever been traded before.

Currency trading is a basic service to bank customers, and banks attend to the foreign currency needs of their government or corporate clients in order to build better business ties with them. Currency traders also earn commissions, of course. The business is safe, for the bank is simply matching buyers with sellers, exchanging, for example, its customer's dollars for someone else's yen. Banks willing to take more risks can bet their own money on "open positions," holding a currency that they have purchased and hoping it will go up in value. The unpredictability of currency markets makes this an uncertain proposition, but well-managed currency trading—or "forex (foreign exchange) trading," in the market jargon—can be quite profitable. In 1985, Citibank's investment banking arm made four-fifths of its profits from trading-related activities.

As the offshore markets have developed and telecommunications technology has advanced, foreign exchange markets have become huge and global. In fact, since money moves easily among financial markets around the world, foreign exchange trading now continues twenty-four hours a day. When the New York foreign exchange markets close, those in Australia are just opening; a few hours later Tokyo and Singapore open, then Bahrain, Frankfurt, and London, then New York again. During each twenty-four-hour cycle, tens of billions of dollars are traded for marks, francs, pounds, and other currencies.

Unlike stocks, bonds, and commodities, foreign currencies are not generally traded in physical marketplaces. Phone and telex wires link buyers and sellers of foreign exchange, and the traders could as easily be across the street as around the world. Each major financial institution has its own foreign-exchange trading room, linked to its customers, to its brokers (who execute the deals), and to the trading rooms of its counterparts.

A forex trading room resembles a video arcade. A trading room has banks of electronic "desks," at each of which sits a trader. In front of the trader is a set of video display terminals with the latest market information. Next to the terminals is a telephone, with fifty or sixty buttons by it, each providing direct contact with a major customer or another trading room. Push the button marked "BA," for example, and you're talking to the trader for Bank of America. Two or three more single-line phones on the desk are connected to the bank's brokers, and a few more video display terminals scattered around the trading room read out either more general or more specific market information. When traders sit at their desks they see a constant display of market quotes and a bank of telephone lines that connect them to the rest of the market.

Against the walls are rows of telex terminals that print everything from world news to communications from clients. Next to the trading room is an operations room, where the dealers' verbal agreements are committed to paper and formalized. Telexes clatter, phones ring, and excited traders shout into two or three phone receivers at a time.

When markets are volatile, traders are in a state of near-frenzy, trying to close deals even as prices change. Few are over thirty-five, since fifteen years in a trading room is enough to permanently frazzle anyone's nerves. The head trader or trading room manager patrols the aisles, checking on the action at the various desks. Each trader specializes in one currency, or two or more if the currency is "exotic"—minor in volume, like the Finnish markka or the Greek drachma. The trader's specialty is sometimes marked by a small national flag of that currency above the desk—the Union Jack for pounds sterling, the tricolor for francs, and so on.

The room looks chaotic but runs with precision. Each trader watches the market, stays in touch with other dealers in that currency, closes the deals he or she is called upon to negotiate, and sends the paperwork on to a platoon of clerks.

In hundreds of trading rooms around the world the delicate balance between chaos and order is maintained, and foreign exchange markets move smoothly up and down.

A few hours in the trading room of a New York bank will give an idea of how the market works. On this day the forex markets have been jumpy and thin—that is, there is great uncertainty about their direction and few of the big speculators are willing to bet one way or another. The dollar has been rising steadily for months, in apparent defiance of all economic principles, and it might begin to fall again at any time. To make matters more complex, a few days before, the Bundesbank, the German central bank, intervened in the market, buying marks to keep the mark from declining any further against the dollar. Traders, speculators, and normal clients are all wondering whether the long-awaited dollar drop has come.

On this morning the New York market is nervous. Al Warner is the Deutsche mark trader here, and there has been almost no action since the market opened. On the screen in front of him are seven or eight currency quotes; Warner focuses on the following line:

DM   Citi   3.0875/95   55/75   3.0920/40   3.0840/60

Warner knows, then, that Citibank, a market leader, is willing to sell German marks (Deutsche marks or DM) at 3.0875 to the dollar (or 32.39 cents per mark); it is willing to buy them at 3.0895 to the dollar (or 32.37 cents per mark). The difference, 0.0020 marks or .02 cents, known to traders as "twenty pips," is the bid/offer spread—the difference between what Citibank will buy and what it will sell marks for. The twenty-pip spread is large, two or three times the usual, which means that in its uncertainty Citibank is trying to discourage business by charging a stiff markup. Warner looks at the next column, which tells him that the most recent previous price quote was 3.0855/75, so the mark is declining against the dollar. (The more marks there are to the dollar, the weaker the mark is.) The next two columns show the high (3.0920/40) and low (3.0840/60) quotes for the day so far. From these, Warner can see that the mark has been fairly constant all day.

As new price quotes come in, the screen changes. At the bottom of the screen, news flashes alert traders to economic or political events that might affect currency values, such as a government crisis or a rise in the inflation rate. With the push of a button, Warner can get more details on any one of a number of news items coming off the Reuter's wire, the market's leading electronic news service.

It is a few minutes to 11:00 A.M. in New York, which means that the European markets are about to close and the action will shift here. In fact, two or three minutes after Europe closes, as the traders put it, the dollar begins to drop and the DM to rise. That is, the current quote goes from 3.0875/95 to 3.0855/75 to 3.0825/55 and continues to drop. (These changes may seem small, but for a corporation trying to sell $100 million, a rise in the DM from 3.09 to 3.08 means a loss of over $300,000. Although the price change may be just three-tenths of 1 percent, there are very few prices that can change so much all over the world in the space of a couple of minutes.)

As the dollar declines, Warner's screen flashes to indicate that a news story has broken. Warner hits a button and the screen informs him that just before Europe closed rumors hit the market that the Bundesbank had intervened, buying marks to raise their price. Warner looks perplexed, and turns to head trader Rob Giuliano; they exchange a few words and agree that the rumor is probably unfounded. Yet the DM keeps rising.

Al Warner's phone board lights up in an unusual place;

someone overseas is calling. It is Andreas Karistos in Athens, an occasional customer who deals for a large Greek shipping firm. Karistos is nervous; he is holding lots of dollars and does not want to get caught by a big drop in their value.

"What's the mark trading at there?" Karistos asks Warner.

Warner looks at his screen, which is showing new quotes every couple of seconds, generally around 3.0800. He tells Karistos to hold on, then Warner picks up the phone that puts him through to his broker.

"What are marks?" Warner barks; no formalities are required. Warner's broker tells him that right now the quote he's dealing at is 3.0815/35. Warner relays the information to Karistos. Karistos is worried, asks a few more questions, and then makes his decision. He wants to sell dollars and buy 200 million marks.

Warner now has his marching orders: Buy 200 million marks with dollars at the lowest possible price, as soon as possible. This is a big order, nearly $70 million, and Karistos is a valued customer, so Warner is pleased. Yet he is also in a bind. Warner has to buy Karistos' marks without upsetting the market. If Warner were to try to buy DM 200 million all at once, the price of the mark would rise as soon as the news got to the very nervous market, and Karistos would be forced either to withdraw or to pay inflated prices for his marks. If Warner were to buy only a few million marks an hour, the market would be unaffected, but with the mark rising gradually anyway, this seems a bad gamble.

Meanwhile the dollar is in free-fall. It is 11:30 A.M., and the mark is up to 3.05 or so; from the 32.4 cents a mark cost an hour ago, it is up to 32.8 cents, a rise of 1.3 percent in an hour. This is a great deal by currency-market standards. It means, among other things, that the West German economy is now 1.3 percent larger in dollar terms than it was an hour ago, a gain of over $7 billion. The bid-offer spread is fifty or sixty pips, indicating that even the big banks, the "market makers" who stand ready to buy or sell marks at all times, are unwilling to deal.

Warner thinks for a moment, glances over at Rob Giuliano, then punches the button to take Karistos off hold. "Andreas, listen. The market's real skittish right now. We're going to have to do it in dribs and drabs or we'll take it on the chin."

Andreas is noncommittal, and Rob Giuliano whispers to Warner that the Greek's English probably does not include such expressions as "dribs and drabs," and "take it on the chin." Warner tries again in simpler terms, and Karistos now agrees. Warner will try to buy marks in small quantities, inconspicuously, without raising the price of the mark and making the deal more expensive. Warner tells Karistos to stay on the line and begins operating.

The mark is now hovering around 3.05, as Warner listens carefully for any trader who might need to sell a small number of marks. One telex is giving the room the news that rumors of Bundesbank intervention are rife, and there is even speculation that the Fed, America's central bank, is also intervening. Warner asks one of his junior traders to call a friend in the Fed's trading room across town, where the rumor is flatly denied. Warner sees an opening and offers to buy marks and sell "two bucks"—$2 million, at 3.0420. The deal is accepted; Warner marks the information down on a notepad and tells the other trader to confirm by telex.

Bit by bit, as the mark continues to fluctuate, Warner places his orders. Three bucks here, five bucks there—each "buck" being a million dollars paid for marks. Andreas Karistos is on the line all the while, and Warner keeps him informed of his progress.

"Andreas, we've got about one-third of your order. It's going very slow. Any faster and we'd be driving the price up.

Do you want to keep trying or wait a while?" Karistos is worried and confused. The mark has continued to rise, now to 3.03/dollar, and every passing minute means money lost to Karistos. He tells Warner to try to buy more.

Warner looks for more deals and tries to talk them up a little. "Two bucks? How about three? Four? O.K. Confirm by telex, please." Fifteen more minutes go by, as Karistos gets more and more nervous. The mark is still rising, as Warner tries to explain to the Greek that any bigger buying will just drive the price up; patience is essential.

By this time the senior vice-president in charge of the trading room is by Al Warner's shoulder. Warner has completed more than half the order, but still needs about DM 80 million ($27 million). Karistos is getting jumpier by the minute, and although the mark seems to have settled around 3.0300, Athens wants to complete its purchase. Giuliano, Warner, and the senior executive confer. They, unlike Karistos, think the dollar's decline is spent and that the dollar will soon start to rise again. If Karistos will only wait, the marks he wants will get cheaper.

"Andreas," Warner tells Athens, "the thing seems to have stopped. We think the mark'll be coming back a little. When? Can't tell, maybe half an hour or so."

Karistos is still nervous. The executive checks the board once more, confirms the general opinion that the dollar will soon rise, then decides that if Karistos is not willing to take a chance, the bank will. The bank itself will sell Karistos the remaining marks at the current rate. The impatient customer will get his marks without upsetting the market. Meanwhile, the bank bets that the dollar will rise and that it will be able to buy the marks more cheaply. Only the executive can decide this, since it involves the bank taking a $27 million "open position." Up until now, Al Warner has simply been operating for Karistos, and every mark that

Warner bought has been passed on to Athens. If Karistos bails out, he will have his marks and the bank will be gambling with its own money.

Warner puts Athens back on the line. "Andreas, we'll buy the rest from you at 3.03. There's about $27 million left. Yes, we'll give the rest to you if you don't want to wait. If you wait a while we can still try to deal. No? O.K., so you're all set."

Now Warner is dealing with the bank's money. The bank has sold Andreas Karistos marks at 3.03/dollar, so that any marks Warner can buy more cheaply are bank profit. Warner sits back and places his lunch order with a nearby deli. It is now 12:15 P.M.

The mark hits 3.0250/70 and then begins to drop. By 12:30 the mark is under 3.03 again and weakening. It gets close to 3.04 and Warner begins to buy.

"What are marks? Thanks." Off that line.

"Three bucks? Make it four? Five? Great, confirm by telex. Thank you."

By 12:45 Warner's notepad is full. The bank has bought about 82 million marks at an average price of 3.04 for resale to Karistos at 3.03. The difference—nearly $90,000—is the bank's profit on the deal, along with whatever commission Karistos will pay. Warner, of course, is beaming.

"Sorry, Andreas," he mutters as he leans back contentedly in his chair, relaxed for the first time in two hours. Warner hasn't cheated Karistos, who, after all, didn't have the nerves or the faith in his instincts to take such a big chance. Indeed, Karistos was able to bail out when he wanted to and got his marks at a decent price. The $90,000 he sacrificed by selling out early to Warner was worth the peace of mind; Karistos is no gambler.

Andreas Karistos has sold over $65 million for marks, two-thirds *through* Al Warner, the rest directly *to* him. Warner has placed orders for DM 200 million, two-thirds on Karistos' account and the rest for the bank, to be resold to Karistos. Warner's trading day is over; this is a big enough deal for him to ignore the market for the rest of the afternoon.

Although Al Warner's day is over, the money he has been trading has just begun to move. When Warner completes his transactions, he sends tickets with a few details of the trades to the "back office," or operations room. Clerks there, perhaps aided by details supplied in telexes from the parties selling the marks, draw up standard contracts between buyer and sellers specifying the price and the way in which the marks and dollars will be traded. This is no simple matter: Karistos cannot simply deliver $65 million in dollar bills in return for 200 million Deutsche mark notes. Funds must be moved across a number of borders, upon electronic or cable instruction, from and to bank accounts around the world. Karistos instructs his bank to transfer the requisite number of dollars into the bank accounts of the dollars' buyers, while they in turn instruct their banks to shift a corresponding amount in marks to Karistos' account.

Karistos' deal is a minuscule part of the normal day's foreign exchange trading. Daily volume on the world's foreign exchange market is now about $200 billion, and the volume is doubling every five years or so. One-third of these transactions are channeled through London, a quarter through New York, one-tenth each through Zurich and Frankfurt; most of the rest is carried out in Tokyo, Singapore, and Hong Kong. Only a tiny fraction of this foreign exchange trading is needed for actual trade in goods—annual world trade is equal to about three weeks of forex activity—and most of it represents lightning movements into and out of currencies in response to small changes in their real or expected values.

International bankers have devised streamlined ways to carry out these long-distance electronic fund transfers, which are so common and so important to world trade and investment. Payment instructions between North American and European banks are sent by the Brussels-based Society for Worldwide Interbank Financial Telecommunications, known as SWIFT. The computer-based SWIFT transfer network does electronically and more or less instantaneously what used to require cabled instructions and confirmations. Dollars sent from London to New York and back, or marks sent from London to Frankfurt and back, are transmitted by SWIFT in split seconds. In fact, SWIFT transfers hundreds of billions of dollars back and forth between banks and bank customers every day.

In New York, funds are transferred through a similar interbank system known as the Clearing House Interbank Payments System, or CHIPS. All the world's big international banks are members of CHIPS or have correspondent ties to a member bank. Through CHIPS the world's major banks transfer dollars back and forth, both for their customers and on their own. Generally speaking, Eurodollar transfers go through CHIPS; that is, offshore operations involving dollars are routed through the CHIPS mechanism. This helps explain the incredible size of the system; on an average business day, CHIPS handles over 70,000 deals, with an average size of $3 million each for a total of over $200 billion a day. In three days, more dollars go through CHIPS than there are dollars in the money supply of the United States.

The efficiency with which the offshore markets carry out their everyday errands allows them to connect money markets around the world. Short-term interest rates and currency values are determined in one global trading room joined by the latest in telecommunications technology. If the Fed announces an unexpected and unwelcome increase in the American money supply, thousands of traders all over the world reach for their telephones and hit the buttons on their control panels. Within minutes millions of dollars change hands in thousands of simultaneous transactions, gradually bidding the price of the currency down. In this world of offshore markets and instantaneous transoceanic funds transfers, national boundaries mean very little.

Long-term lending is the core of international banking. Offshore banks channel hundreds of billions of dollars a year from investors and depositors to borrowers. The Euromarket is a global arbiter of international creditworthiness, funding firms or governments whose programs it finds attractive and ignoring those it disapproves of. The international financial system is thus a central determinant of worldwide economic trends.

The Euromarkets, like all banking systems, must attract deposits. Offshore banks, in fact, offer rates that national banking systems can seldom match, because they have few regulatory constraints and deal entirely in large quantities, which saves on overhead. Eurodollar deposits pay from ½ to 2 percent more than similar accounts in the United States; three-month Eurodollar bank certificates of deposit (CDs) pay ¼ to ½ percent more than three-month CDs in the United States. An added attraction for some overseas depositors, especially from the East and Mideast, is the geographic and legal distance of the funds from fickle national authorities.

The offshore centers hold well over a trillion dollars in investors' money. Although accurate figures on the depositors are not available, it is often guessed that two-thirds of the money comes from the advanced industrialized nations, one-sixth from OPEC, and one-sixth from other developing countries. About a third of the depositors are multinational corporations whose sales and production are as international as the offshore markets and who need ready access to various currencies. Another third are governments, especially from the Third World (including OPEC). Most of the remainder comes from large institutional investors, who are drawn by yields, and from private investors, who are drawn by both yields and secrecy. As much as one-quarter of the money Americans invest in money-market mutual funds goes directly to the offshore markets, and more finds its way there indirectly. Private citizens—frightened Latin Americans, wealthy Kuwaitis, tax-shy Europeans, and concerned Americans—place part of their portfolio with bank branches in Luxembourg, the Bahamas, London, and Hong Kong.

The money that floods into the offshore markets from around the world is, of course, lent out. The offshore markets entice borrowers for many of the same reasons that they attract investors. Interest rates are generally lower than in national markets, so that many American corporations, for example, can borrow dollars more cheaply on the Euromarkets than the U.S. government can within the United States. Huge deals can be made quickly and with little paperwork; Eurobankers boast of putting together billion dollar loans over a long weekend. The great speed of Euromarket bank lending is largely owing to widespread use of "syndication," in which a group of banks cooperate to float a loan.

Syndicated Euromarket bank loans are put together typically by a small management group of banks, who recruit a larger group of banks to participate once the deal is negotiated. The loans are at a floating interest rate, much as are adjustable-rate mortgages in the United States. The baseline used for most Eurocredits is the three- or six-month London Interbank Offering Rate, or LIBOR: the rate at which banks in London borrow from each other. A very reliable borrower might pay a "spread" of one-quarter of a percentage point above LIBOR, while a less creditworthy borrower might pay LIBOR plus 2 percent. The loan's interest rate is usually adjusted upward or downward, as LIBOR changes, every six months. The average Eurocurrency loan gives the borrower seven years to repay.

A Eurocredit might begin with a meeting between the finance minister of South Korea and representatives of six international banks. The South Koreans and their bankers discuss the purpose of the loan, and the country's economic conditions, and figure out how much the market might be willing to lend and at what "spread" above LIBOR. The six-bank group—the "lead managers"—draw up a contract specifying the terms of the loan and bargain with the South Koreans. Once agreement is reached—let us say, for $500 million for eight years at a spread of 1 percent above LIBOR—the lead managers must try to bring other banks into the deal. The six lead managers decide who will approach which other banks; for example, the French bank Credit Commercial de France, known as CCF, might be assigned the Chase Manhattan Bank. Then CCF in Paris sends Chase's London offices a telex:

> De Credit Commercial de France
> A Chase Manhattan Bank N.A. London
> Attention: Monsieur Peter Sachs
> Re: International Syndication
> US Dollars 500 Million Loan to the Republic of Korea
>
> The undersigned lead-management group has been requested and authorized by the Republic of Korea to arrange a credit facility on their behalf.
> We are pleased to invite your bank to join this transaction as either a co-lead manager with an initial underwriting commitment of US dollars 30 million or a manager with an initial underwriting commitment of US dollars 15 million.

CCF, on behalf of the six banks that arranged the half-billion-dollar loan, is offering Chase participation as co-lead manager, a step below the lead managers, or as manager, two steps below. The telex presents the details of participation:

The basic terms and conditions of the loan are set out below:

Borrower	Republic of Korea
Amount	US Dollars 500 Million
Purpose of Borrowing	To finance the cost of projects detailed in the information memorandum
Final Maturity	8 years from the date of signing of the loan agreement
Availability Period	18 months from the date of signature of the loan
Interest Rate	1% per annum above the rate offered for 6-month deposits in dollars
Repayment	In 9 equal semiannual installments commencing 48 months from the date of signature of the loan agreement
Prepayment	Permitted on any interest payment date subject to 30 days' prior notice and in minimum amount of US dollars 50 million (or multiples thereof)

This tells Chase's Monsieur Sachs how the South Koreans will pay for their $500 million. The loan's maturity, the period within which it is to be repaid, is eight years. It can be drawn upon at any time within the next eighteen months, and principal payments will start in four years. The interest rate is 1 percent above the six-month Eurodollar deposit rate, the London Interbank Offering Rate, or LIBOR. Every six months, when interest payments are calculated, they will be set at 1 percent above LIBOR—13 percent if LIBOR is 12 percent, 10 percent if LIBOR is 9 percent, and so on.

Chase is a major bank, and its participation in the loan might help attract other potential lenders. CCF and the South Koreans therefore offer Chase some incentives to join the syndicate. The more prominently Chase agrees to participate, the more incentives Chase receives:

Commitment Fee 1   For co-lead managers which commit themselves with an underwriting amount of US
dollars 30 million:
—an underwriting fee of ⅛% flat on the
underwriting commitment
—a participation fee of ⅝% flat on the final
participation

Commitment Fee 2   For managers which commit themselves
with an underwriting amount of US dollars
15 million:
—an underwriting fee of ¹⁄₁₆% flat on the
underwriting commitment
—a participation fee of ⅝% flat on the final
participation

CCF and the other five initiators of the loan are the "lead managers"; their names appear first in the public announcement of the loan. Any other bank willing to commit itself to $30 million will be a "co-lead manager" and will receive fees totaling $225,000 in addition to normal interest payments. Then come the simple "managers"—banks lending $15 million and receiving a bit over $100,000 in fees. Smaller amounts still—too small to interest Chase—bring ever smaller upfront, or "front-end," fees.

CCF gives the final details of the offering and signs off:

Documentation   This transaction shall be subject to
the negotiations, execution, and de-
livery of a mutually satisfactory loan
documentation in the form of a
standard Eurodollar agreement

Agent Bank   National Westminster Bank, Ltd.

Governing Law   Laws of England

Information Memorandum   An Information Memorandum
from which is extracted the sum-
mary of economic data on the Republic of Korea (see below) is available on request. It will detail the

projects to be financed by this credit.

The telex ends with a term sheet explaining the loan's conditions, and with a summary of economic data. Over the next few days Peter Sachs, Chase's loan officer for the Far East, consults Chase's economic and political analysts about South Korea. He makes sure that the bank has not surpassed its internal Korean "country exposure limit," which sets the upper boundary the bank wants to commit to borrowers in each country. Sachs might check with the manager of Chase's branch in Seoul, South Korea, and call a few friends at other international banks. He has to get approval for the loan from the bank's credit committee, composed of a battery of executive and senior vice-presidents. If the rates are reasonable, the bank has the funds available, and its experts consider South Korea relatively safe, Chase will participate as a "co-lead manager" for $30 million.

When enough banks join the lending syndicate to provide the $500 million, the banks and the South Korean government sign a loan contract. A tombstone—a public announcement listing all the participating banks—appears in one of the trade publications of international finance, such as the *Financial Times* or *Euromoney*. South Korea has borrowed half a billion dollars.

Syndicated Euromarket bank loans are unlike previous forms of international lending. In the past, large long-term lending, whether international or domestic, was usually done on bond markets. If General Motors or Poland wanted to borrow capital, they hired an investment bank to arrange for a bond issue. The investment bank set an interest rate it believed the market would bear and sold the bonds to investors. A $100 million loan might have been divided into 100,-000 smaller pieces, each one a $1,000 bond, and sold to wealthy individuals, insurance companies, small savers, and other investors.

Today's syndicated bank credits also lend out the money of many small savers, but unlike the past, the savers' permission is not required. An investor in the 1920s who bought a bond of General Motors or the Polish government did so consciously, presumably aware of the relevant risks and return. When a consortium of American, British, German, and Japanese banks lends money to General Motors or Poland today, it is using the deposits of millions of Americans, Britons, Germans, and Japanese, but does not have to consult with them. There is nothing illegal or unethical about this; the role of banks is to put the money they are entrusted with to its most lucrative use and to pass along some of the earnings to their depositors. Banks that lend internationally do so because they expect that both they and their depositors will benefit as a result.

There are advantages to syndicated bank credits rather than bonds. Reducing the numbers of lenders streamlines transactions. Instead of satisfying thousands of small bondholders whose fears or enthusiasm may be groundless, borrowers from a bank syndicate have only to win the confidence of a handful of bankers who spend all their time following the market and are presumably better informed than the proverbial bond-buying widows and pensioners.

Should the borrower run into difficulty, syndicated bank loans may make it easier to avoid financial panic than bond-based foreign lending did in the past. When most foreign loans were by bondholders, the slightest hint that the debtor might have trouble maintaining prompt interest and principal payments characteristically led to something like a bank run. Each individual bondholder had an incentive to sell out immediately, before the debtor's credit rating collapsed and while its bonds were still worth something. The ensuing rush to sell questionable bonds exacerbated the problem, as confidence cascaded downward along with the price of the debtor's bonds. Because there were thousands, even millions, of bondholders, it was nearly impossible for the debtor in question to attempt to negotiate a mutually acceptable settlement. Bondholders and investment banks sometimes set up committees to represent the bondholders in such negotiations, but there was still room for financial panics that rapidly became self-reinforcing. Since syndicated Eurocurrency credits are offered by small groups of at most a hundred banks, and led by even smaller management groups, negotiations between creditors and debtors are not so difficult.

Bank loan syndication can allow lenders to coordinate their actions more effectively, but it may also have pernicious effects. The handful of banks involved in international lending today may have a far greater potential for self-reinforcing delusions or illusions than millions of scattered bondholders. When Henrik Ibsen observed that "these heroes of finance are like beads on a string: when one slips off, all the rest follow,"[7] he might well have been describing the herd instinct that sometimes dominates Eurobanking. The international financial markets are so exclusive, and so inbred, that stampedes by international bankers who think very much alike, in whatever direction, are not uncommon. Rumors that a debtor country or company is in trouble might ricochet around the very closed world of Eurobanking rapidly and convincingly enough to lead banks to stop new lending or call in existing short-term credits. On a number of occasions these stampedes have had consequences not very distinguishable from those of financial panics by small investors.

International bank loans also expose entire national financial systems, rather than a few bondholders, to the risk inherent in international lending. Bondholders know the risks when they buy bonds, and if a company or country defaults on its bonds, only the bondholders suffer the immediate consequences. But a default on a bank loan, by contrast, endangers millions of small checking and savings accounts. If these deposits are insured by national governments, as they often are, default on a major bank loan might force taxpayers and unsuspecting customers of the bank to bear part of the burden for the bank's poor judgments.

Because there are disadvantages as well as advantages to syndicated Eurocredits, international banks also arrange for bond issues on the offshore markets. Like a bank loan, a Eurobond is negotiated by the borrower with a group of underwriting banks, but the bonds are sold to investors. About $150 billion in Eurobonds are issued every year, approximately one-half of all medium- and long-term international lending. About half of all Eurobond buyers, it is estimated, are private individuals, and most of the rest are such institutional investors as pension funds and investment trusts. Bond markets tend to be more cautious than banks, and only the most reliable of corporations and governments can sell Eurobonds successfully.

On the Euromarkets, the world's most important banks bring the world's most powerful investors together with the world's leading corporations and governments. Every year hundreds of billions of dollars in syndicated Eurocurrency bank credits, Eurobonds, and a variety of more exotic financial instruments are made available to borrowers all over the world. As the international banking system moves this huge mass of capital from source to use, it can affect the fate of firms, industries, and even countries.

In some ways the great size and practical extraterritoriality of the offshore markets allows them virtually to dictate economic policies to the world's governments. A policy that reduces international financial confidence in the prospects for the national economy, for example, will lead investors to get their capital out of the country and foreign exchange traders to sell the local currency. The effects of the capital outflow and a run on the currency can be far more disastrous than whatever problems the original policy was meant to confront.

The ability of the contemporary international financial system to shift billions of dollars from place to place in minutes gives the markets something akin to veto power over domestic or international decisions. All the world's companies and governments are interested in having access to funds as cheaply as possible. The great integration of contemporary financial markets means that this battle for finance is global; companies and governments compete against each other for the confidence of the international financial system. Actions that reduce confidence will raise the cost of capital to firms or countries, so they must be concerned with maintaining the markets' goodwill.

For international bankers, the markets' ability to restrain the behavior of politicians is a profoundly good thing. International finance thrives in large part because national governments do not interfere with it. More generally, the international financial system depends so entirely on the free movement of capital across borders that any attempt to restrict these movements is a threat to the markets as they are currently organized. The international financial community, then, has a vested interest in convincing the world's governments, and their people, that intervention in their business will be counterproductive, and may even be impossible. This does not mean that bankers' opinions are dishonest—or even that they are incorrect—only that, as John Quincy Adams once said of Czar Alexander I, the average banker "finds a happy coincidence between the dictates of his conscience and the needs of his Empire."

Walter Wriston is the most prominent spokesperson for the American international banking community, and there is little doubt that his conscience coincides with his needs. In the decade up to 1984, Wriston was one of the world's leading bankers as chairman and chief executive officer of Citibank. He helped engineer Citibank's extraordinary international expansion in the 1970s, and even in retirement he is a participant in efforts to keep world markets open. He has earned praise from economist and militant free-marketeer Milton Friedman, for whom Wriston's "independence of thought, intellectual integrity, and foresighted vision" make him "the most innovative banker of our time," and from conservative Republican Congressman Jack Kemp, who calls Wriston "one of America's sharpest and most creative minds."[8]

Wriston believes that the battle between markets and politics is nearly over, and that politicians have already lost to what he calls "the information standard"—the ability of firms and individuals to communicate globally and instantaneously. Wriston spoke to me in his Citicorp Center Office:

> The gold standard, replaced by the gold exchange standard, which was replaced by the Bretton Woods arrangements, has now been replaced by the information standard. Unlike the other standards, the information standard is in place, operating, will never go away, and has substantially changed the world. What it means, very simply, is that bad monetary and fiscal policies anywhere in the world are reflected within minutes on the Reuters screens in the trading rooms of the world.
>
> Money only goes where it's wanted, and only stays where it's well treated, and once you tie the world together with telecommunications and information, the ball game is over. It's a new world, and the fact is, the information standard is more draconian than any gold standard. They think the gold standard was tough. All you had to do on the gold standard was renounce it; we proved that. You cannot renounce the information standard, and it is exerting a discipline on the countries of the world,

which they all hate. For the first time in history, the politicians can't stop it. It's beyond the political control of the world, and that's the good news.

The size and speed of today's international financial transactions, Wriston says, makes it impossible for politicians to override the market's judgment.

There's not enough money in the world to support a currency with dumb fiscal and monetary management. The president of the United States goes out in the Rose Garden and says something dumb. The trading lights of the world light up, and it's all over. In France, Mitterrand announced all those ridiculous moves, and they lost a third of their foreign exchange in a week.

There are 60,000-odd terminals out there in the trading rooms of the world, and those guys are about as sentimental as a block of ice. If they're going to sell, that's it. This is new in the history of the world, and I don't think it can be structured or contained, and I think that's good news over a longer time frame. There's no place to hide.

Wriston realizes that market signals can be uncomfortable for political leaders or systems.

The last thing the political process wants is to be accountable. But there's nothing the politicians can do. The information standard, the information-intensive society, moves accountability from a few knowledgeable men and women to the population. Internationally, it moves it to a judgment of the way your policies look to the international markets.

At the end of the day, it's a new world and the concept of sovereignty is going to change. Politically, the new world is an integrated market in which nobody can get away with what they used to. You can't control what your people hear, you can't control the value of your currency, you can't control your capital flows. The idea of fifteenth-century international law is gone. It hasn't laid down yet, but it's dead. It's like the three-mile limit in a world of Inter-Continental Ballistic Missiles.

Wriston's logic is compelling in many regards. The offshore markets are so efficient at moving money that billions of dollars can travel halfway around the world in a matter of minutes. If French interest rates go up a notch, billions can move into the franc; if the government falls in Italy, trillions of lire can be sold by concerned corporations and investors. If the Hong Kong offshore market looks unsteady, billions can move to Singapore; if the Singapore market strengthens, billions can leave London for the Strait of Malacca.

Wriston implies that contemporary international finance is nearly divorced from national governments, and indeed he might like it to be so. Certainly the remarkable advances in modern electronics since 1960 have magnified the impact global markets have on national policies. In addition, the international financial system derives great power from the peculiar nature of the offshore markets, which are far more difficult to manipulate politically than national markets.

Nevertheless, the Euromarkets are not stateless; they rest on the implicit, and sometimes explicit, support of major Western governments. The offshore markets arose, after all, in response to actions by national governments, and they grew because national governments tolerated or encouraged them. At any point in the last thirty years, the U.S. government could have put a stop to much Euromarket activity by prohibiting American banks from participating and by blocking the use of the U.S. dollar offshore. The costs of such a step would undoubtedly have been very high, and the American authorities felt no need for such action, but the fact that it was and remains possible illustrates how the offshore markets thrive on the sufferance of the home governments of major banks and currencies.

The interrelationship of the offshore markets and the major Western governments was underlined by the world financial crises of 1974 and 1982–1983. The crises were overcome only when the home governments of offshore banks agreed to bolster the international financial markets. In both instances the markets themselves would probably have come close to collapse without government intervention.

In 1974, trouble began when two mid-sized Euromarket banks failed. In the summer and early autumn, the German Bankhaus I. D. Herstatt and Long Island's Franklin National Bank collapsed. Both Herstatt and Franklin speculated heavily and disastrously in foreign exchange markets, tried to disguise losses from national authorities, and eventually both went bankrupt. When Herstatt went under in June 1974, the West German authorities insisted on a thorough audit before they would make good on the bank's offshore commitments. As a result, a number of foreign currency transactions that were "in the pipeline" got frozen. Morgan Guaranty Trust Co. of New York, for example, had sold and delivered Deutsche marks to Herstatt, which Herstatt was to pay for in dollars the next day, but in the meantime the bank failed, the German government froze all transfers, and Morgan did not receive the dollars it had contracted for. Banks immediately appealed to their governments for relief.

Franklin National was far larger than Herstatt, and the potential for disaster was far greater.[9] In 1972, Italian financier Michele Sindona bought control of the Long Island bank. He immediately set about using Franklin for massive foreign exchange speculation; the bank's daily currency trading went from under $20 million in 1971 to $3.8 billion at the end of 1973. The bank lost heavily, and compounded incompetence with fraud to cover up its true position. By May 1974, Franklin was near collapse, and after five months of gradual disintegration the bank closed and was bought by European American Bank, a consortium of European financial institutions. Like the Herstatt failure, Franklin's demise raised serious doubts about the reliability of normal foreign exchange markets.

The two major bank failures in 1974 threw the currency

and interbank markets into panic. If day-to-day foreign currency and other fund transfers were not safe, the offshore markets were useless. Large banks practically refused to deal with smaller banks whose failure was at all possible, and the interbank market actually shrank in the last half of 1974. Foreign exchange trading volume dropped by almost two-thirds.

Concerted action by national governments eventually controlled the damage caused by the 1974 crisis and allowed the offshore markets to resume normal operations. When Franklin failed the Federal Reserve, America's central bank, announced that it would take responsibility for Franklin's international commitments. Eventually the German central bank reimbursed Herstatt's creditors. In the months that followed, the world's major central banks agreed to keep a somewhat closer watch on their banks abroad. Since then a semiformal arrangement has evolved that commits governments to supervise their banks offshore and to support the activities of these banks in case of crisis.

In the summer of 1982, the disturbance was more widespread and more serious. Mexico, one of the world's leading borrowers, approached economic collapse. The desperate Mexican government attempted to pull back from disaster, and declared a unilateral freeze in payments on its foreign debt. The Euromarkets, haunted by visions of falling financial dominos, quickly ceased lending to most of Latin America. By the end of 1983, most of the continent's debtors were renegotiating their existing debts as the debtors reached one stage or another of financial disintegration.

The Reagan administration originally insisted that the debt crisis was a private matter between the debtors and the banks. It soon decided, however, that the shock waves from a Latin American financial collapse would endanger the American financial system itself. The country's largest banks had loaned tens of billions of dollars to Latin America, and if these loans were not serviced, the most important banks in the United States might fail. Indeed, by 1982 outstanding American loans to the five largest Latin American debtors— Mexico, Brazil, Argentina, Venezuela, and Chile—were larger than the total capital of the United States' entire banking system.

The threat of a major financial panic drove the Reagan administration to act. The Federal Reserve System, the Treasury, and other U.S. government agencies stepped in to help Mexico, Brazil, and Argentina over their roughest spots. The International Monetary Fund and the Bank for International Settlements spent months in arduous struggle to avoid an international financial collapse. With the help of tens of billions of dollars of aid provided by American and Western European taxpayers, panic was again avoided. Large loans were extended to the troubled debtors so that they could continue to meet interest payments, and the International Monetary Fund negotiated stabilization programs to restructure the debtors' economies. As international financial turmoil began to affect the American banking system, the U.S. government again stood ready to keep the machinery running. When one of the nation's largest banks, Continental Illinois, was weakened by bad loans and forced into collapse when overseas depositors withdrew their funds, the government nationalized the bank to avoid a broader panic.

The 1974 and 1982–1983 financial crises demonstrate that international financial markets are not so stateless as international bankers such as Walter Wriston might believe or desire. National governments were essential to overcoming the possibilities for panic inherent in both episodes, and indeed international bankers were consistent and insistent in their demands that governments step into the financial breach. Governments may need the banks, but the banks also need governments.

Not only does the international financial system depend

on national governments, but it is extremely sensitive to political factors. It is certainly true that the international financial environment has powerful effects on national and international politics, but it is also true that politics affects international financial trends. Financial markets bank on the future, and they rely heavily on expectations that are colored by political developments. The election of a new government widely perceived as pro-business might draw funds into the country and its currency; a new tax code or a new government budget similarly could drive international financial flows. A government that wants to embark on ambitious new investment projects or military spending needs only to convince international bankers of its reliability to be able to borrow the funds it requires, and reliability is a subjective, largely political consideration. In this sense, just as international financial markets may veto national policies, they may also serve as a tool in the implementation of government policies.

For these reasons, some observers question the independence of international financial markets from the policies of national governments. John Heimann's career makes him sympathetic to this view. Heimann has long Wall Street experience and now specializes in international financial matters for Merrill Lynch. In the Carter administration, however, Heimann served as one of the top financial supervisors in the country: he was comptroller of the currency, the Treasury Department's chief bank regulator.

John Heimann sees the world's banks as more or less passive reactors that carry economic and political impulses from market to market. "The properly functioning world financial system," he told me, "is really a transmission system; I don't think it is a critical factor. The political considerations that affect the economies of the world are fundamental. The financial system becomes the victim, the benefactor, or the implementer. But the financial system itself, regardless of the extraordinary arrogance of bankers, really is a secondary consideration. The fiscal and monetary policies of individual countries, whatever they happen to be, will have a greater effect on a bank's profits and losses than the genius of the bank management."

Politics and economics are, in fact, as tightly linked in international finance as they are in the rest of modern society. The modern international financial system is a creature of political decisions, whether those made at Bretton Woods in 1944, those that forced financial markets offshore in the 1960s, or those that kept them from failing in the 1970s and 1980s. The financial system's future depends on future trends in international and domestic politics.

Despite their political origins, the international financial markets are by now a force that no national government can ignore. The response of international banks, bond markets, and foreign currency traders must be considered by national governments as they weigh the costs and benefits of public works, tax reform, monetary policy, and virtually anything else a government might do. Although there is nothing new about politicians having to take into account investor responses to government decisions, the size of today's international financial markets and the speed with which they can react to events have magnified the impact of financial flows on policymaking.

John Heimann, indeed, recognizes that financial integration has had important effects on politics, both within and between nations: "If we have one world anywhere, it is in the financial system. The strength of this is that it becomes less and less in the national interest to hurt somebody else for the glory and the power. Intervention into the system for noneconomic reasons can certainly mess it up, no question about it. Yet what you see out there is just the opposite: an atmosphere of liberalization in virtually all the industrialized countries, for reasons that you have to assume are in their self-interest."

International financial markets react to political stimuli, while political leaders must take into account the ability of modern international financial markets to shift billions of dollars into and out of their jurisdictions at will. National political systems are subject to the often-severe court of international financial opinion, while politics drives much of what happens in international financial markets. The truth is that nobody has yet figured out how to reconcile national political and economic goals with the new international financial realities. In this uncertain environment, individuals, firms, groups, and countries are very largely at the mercy of cross-cutting economic and political forces that are rarely understood. As is so often the case, those most battered are those least able to withstand these powerful pressures. Borrowing countries in the Third World found this out with a vengeance in the 1980s.

5

Lenders and Borrowers

Developing countries in Latin America, Africa, and Asia owe over $600 billion to international banks. Since 1982, debtor after debtor has gone to the brink of default, and the Third World debt crisis has been the most prominent and controversial issue in international finance.

Debt owed by developing countries has broad implications for international politics and the international economy. If developing countries were to simultaneously repudiate their debts, the resulting financial catastrophe would devastate the world economy. Political relations between developed and developing countries, and within the debtor nations, revolve in large part around the debt issue. Strikes, military takeovers, street rebellions, and election campaigns from Seoul to São Paulo and from Santo Domingo to Khartoum have targeted foreign bankers as the chief enemies of the people.

Justifiable concern over the potential for disaster in Third World debt has obscured some of its deeper effects. Food riots and bank failures, after all, make better headlines than a fundamental change in the structure of the world economy. Yet even if the Third World does spiral downward into financial collapse, borrowed money leaves hundreds of impressive industrial projects that are shifting the locus of the world's manufacturing production.

In the last twenty years, the center of industrial dynamism has moved from North America, Western Europe, and Japan to rapidly developing countries in Latin America, Asia, and Africa, and borrowing from the international financial system has dramatically speeded the process. Over a dozen newly industrializing countries borrowed on the Euromarkets to build modern industries and flooded world markets with their manufactured products. The industrialized world now buys many of its videocassette recorders, shoes, auto parts, and clothes from the same countries that owe more than half a trillion dollars to its banks.

Both aspects of developing-country debt—the underlying instability it introduces into international finance, and the major industrial development it financed—are of profound importance to the United States. The Third World debt crisis has forced banks, businesses, and government agencies in the United States to readjust their activities and their balance sheets to avoid serious domestic economic repercussions. Third World debt-financed industrialization has built a cohort of dynamic new manufacturing regions that are exerting increasing competitive pressure on American firms and workers.

The $600 billion that international banks lent to developing countries is both the biggest success of the international financial system and its most serious failure. International banks transferred vast sums to countries that desperately need capital for economic growth. The borrowers invested much of the money in modern industrial projects of international importance. But when more than fifteen years of frenetic Third World bank borrowing came to an abrupt stop in 1982, the crisis shook the foundations of the financial system itself. The political and economic effects of Third World debt are still being felt.

The attractions of foreign loans have long prompted developing countries to borrow abroad. International capital movements have indeed played a major role in the international expansion of capitalism from its early European base to the rest of the world. As England industrialized in the eighteenth century, it relied heavily on capital provided by the wealthy and experienced Amsterdam financial community. The same Amsterdam financiers bankrolled part of the American Revolution and the postrevolutionary reconstruction. British and Continental lending to the United States in the nineteenth century helped to finance the canal- and railroad-building booms that revolutionized the American economy. Latin American states first borrowed in Europe in the 1820s, soon after they won their independence, and they remain important international debtors. At various times countries in eastern and southern Europe and North Africa, as well as Japan, Canada, Australia, and South Africa have all relied on foreign investors for major portions of their investment financing.

Foreign debt has risks, however. First, as in domestic lending, the borrower's future earnings must cover the interest and principal (debt service) payments. Debt-financed investments need to be productive and well managed enough to earn a rate of return higher than the cost of debt service. For example, if a railroad that earns 10 percent on its capital is built with a loan charging 15 percent interest, the burden will soon prove prohibitive. The constraint can be indirect for governments, since a debt-financed project that yields no immediate return—a highway or a port, for example—can in the medium run increase national income and tax revenues enough to pay for itself. Yet money lent to "kleptocracies" such as the Ottoman Empire in the 1860s and Zaire in the 1970s almost immediately disappeared into the pockets of corrupt and inefficient rulers, and led inevitably to defaults.

A second risk in international lending arises because foreign loans are made to borrowers in a currency that is not their own. In addition to the domestic resources to service their debts, international borrowers need the currency the lender requires for payment. Even if a company or government has cash on hand in local currency, it can meet the demands of foreign creditors only if it can get foreign currency, and this depends on the general international performance of the economy as a whole and on the local government's willingness to use scarce foreign exchange to pay foreign financiers. Investors lent dollars and pounds to Italians and Chileans in the 1920s and wanted dollars and pounds, not lire and pesos, in payment. Yet in the 1930s, export prices dropped drastically, railroads and ports whose ability to service their debts depended on exports went broke, and foreign currency earnings dried up. During the Depression most debtor governments had little hard currency—monies used and trusted around the world such as dollars, pounds, and francs; moreover, they had pressing needs that took priority over foreign bondholders.

Political risks also complicate lending across borders. Loans between different national jurisdictions can be impossible to enforce. For example, if a domestic debtor defaults, creditors have legal recourse; but if a foreign debtor defaults, the creditors may have no court they trust to turn to. If a debtor government refuses to service its debts, creditors can hardly foreclose on foreign territory. Creditors have historically found ways to reduce this risk, ranging from gunboat diplomacy to threats of retaliation. Nevertheless, strikes or civil war can make it impossible for governments to service their debts, and new revolutionary regimes may decide to repudiate the debts of their predecessors. In other words, while within one country the only relevant consideration is whether the borrower will be *able* to service its debts, across borders the lender must also be sure that the borrower will be *willing* to make payments.

In nineteenth-century America, corporations and government projects with foreign debts often failed, and the foreigners seldom recouped their losses. In the 1830s, the state of Mississippi borrowed heavily in London to help finance its cotton export boom. Two large bonds got caught in the backwash of the Panic of 1837, and were in default by 1841. After the Civil War, the Northern military administration and its local allies refused to honor the slaveowners' debts; the 1875 Reconstruction Constitution prohibited payment on the pre-Civil War bonds. The 1830s debts are still unpaid, although the London-based Council of the Corporation of Foreign Bondholders regularly sends polite reminders to the governor of Mississippi that "the Council cannot acquiesce in an unjustifiable default merely because it has been successfully maintained for many years." The council's annual report has noted forlornly for decades that "the State of Mississippi does not reply to communications from the Council, but efforts to recover some value for the Bondholders have not been abandoned."[1]

Economic, foreign currency, and political hazards make foreign lending, especially to developing countries, profitable but precarious. Debtors may fail to repay loans because the projects they used the borrowed money for were mismanaged or otherwise misguided. Poor nations are also especially vulnerable to international economic shocks—a rise in the price of their imports, a decline in the price of their exports—that can use up scarce foreign currency and leave creditors in the cold. The political unrest to which developing countries are prone may also interrupt debt service; and if unrest leads to revolution, the new rulers may see little reason to honor the obligations of their erstwhile oppressors. If, on the other hand, all goes well, international debt can benefit both borrower and lender. Loans can be used to increase industrial capacity and export competitiveness, allowing borrowers to grow rapidly and earn enough to repay their debts.

Everything possible went wrong with international lending in the Depression of the 1930s. The global economic collapse made previously profitable projects insolvent, and bankruptcies swept every nation. As international trade and investment plummeted, even solvent debtors could not earn the foreign currency they needed. Economic and foreign currency shocks fed a wave of nationalism from Latin America to Central and Eastern Europe; political protests were often directed at Anglo-American bankers. Defaults followed almost immediately.

After the traumatic Depression-era defaults it took more than thirty years for American investors to show interest in lending to Latin America and to the newer nations of Asia and Africa. Lending to the Less Developed Countries (LDCs) resumed only when the banks felt that economic and political circumstances had changed enough in parts of the Third World that foreign lending might once more be safe and profitable.

By the 1960s, positive signals from the Third World were overshadowing memories of the 1930s. A dozen or so of the more advanced LDCs were growing very rapidly: industrial production in such nations as South Korea, Taiwan, Mexico, and Brazil was doubling every six or seven years. North American and Western European corporations were expressing their confidence in the LDCs: between 1950 and 1966, American multinationals alone set up five thousand new branches in the Third World. Most of the promising investment possibilities in the Third World, especially those in East Asia and Latin America, were safely within an American security perimeter that brooked little anti-Americanism. The economic and political variables for the more advanced LDCs were all encouraging.

Banks from the United States and Western Europe began lending to selected developing countries in the mid-1960s. In 1963, Mexico floated its first overseas bond in fifty years, and over the next decade the country borrowed between $500 million and $1 billion a year. Brazil, another important LDC debtor, increased its foreign borrowing rapidly from $300 million in 1968 to over $3 billion in 1972. By 1973, Mexico and Brazil each owed overseas financiers about $8 billion. Argentina, Peru, Algeria, Iran, the Philippines, and South Korea also became big borrowers.

Robert Pringle, director of the Group of Thirty, a private consultative group made up of thirty of the world's financial leaders, recalls the banks' role in drumming up business in the developing world: "In the late sixties, any hotel you checked into in any kind of decent developing country was full of bankers opening up markets. They were pioneers in a way, and it was an exciting time. Their efforts to get people to take loans, to teach central banks in developing countries what a syndicated loan was and how they could benefit from it, all did a tremendous amount to integrate those countries financially into the rest of the world to a far greater extent than they ever had been before."

The more advanced developing countries were happy to have access to this new and attractive source of foreign capital. About fifteen Third World nations, mostly in Latin America and eastern Asia, grew so rapidly that a new label, Newly Industrializing Countries, with a new acronym, NICs, was coined for them. Bigger factories demanded more electric power, more raw materials, more steel and aluminum, better telecommunications, and new mass transportation to get workers to their jobs. The Euromarkets were willing to lend the NICs the money to round out their industrial structures.

As more and more banks rushed in where they had previously feared to tread, the offshore markets filled with syndicated loans to LDC borrowers. Eager bankers joined each other in extending larger and larger loans in a widening circle of syndication. Originally only the very largest of banks from North America, Western Europe, and Japan were interested in LDC lending, but as the balance sheets of these big banks showed how profitable overseas lending could be, smaller financial institutions joined in. By the late 1970s, thousands of banks were active in LDC lending, and many of them were small and inexperienced in international markets.

Borrowing quickened when OPEC twice increased oil prices, in 1974 and 1979. The flow of OPEC deposits into the offshore markets made finance more readily available, at the same time that such major oil importers as South Korea and Brazil needed more money to pay for their petroleum imports. Important oil exporters, such as Mexico and Venezuela, could use their ever more valuable oil wealth as collateral for borrowing larger sums. During the first oil shock, the non-OPEC developing nations' balance of payments deficits jumped from $15 billion to $47 billion, while their borrowing from foreign banks rose from $10 billion to $15 billion. During the second oil price hike, non-OPEC developing countries' payment deficits went from $42 billion to $88 billion, while their bank borrowing rose from $25 billion to $49 billion in those years.

The debtors, oil shocked or not, Latin American or North African, were eager to borrow to build new factories, power plants, and mines. A portion of the new output of steel, shoes, or soybeans would be exported to cover interest and principal payments. The correlation might be indirect: debt-financed power plants could not export electricity to pay their creditors, but the new electric energy would allow a more general economic expansion to bring more dollars into the country.

Foreign borrowing had important macroeconomic and microeconomic effects. At the level of the firm, government-owned and private companies used overseas loans to fund major new investment projects. The Brazilian, Mexican, and South Korean governments' steel companies, for example, borrowed heavily to build massive new steel mills that could pay for themselves by exporting some of their output. At the macroeconomic level, the inflow of foreign capital allowed the government to run large budget deficits and the country to run large trade deficits. Governments covered their spending with Euromarket borrowing; the chronic Third World gap between imports and exports was bridged by external credits. Of course the loans would have to be repaid eventually, but debtors and creditors were willing to bet that by then the borrowing countries would be wealthy enough to make their debt service payments painlessly.

The process appealed to both bankers and borrowers. Financiers bankrolled NIC investments, industrial growth quickened, and increased exports paid for the original borrowing. Statistics illustrate the story. A dozen countries account for three-quarters of all LDC debt to international banks: five in Latin America (Mexico, Brazil, Argentina, Venezuela, and Chile); five in East Asia (South Korea, the Philippines, Indonesia, Malaysia, and Thailand); and two in the Middle East (Algeria and Turkey). With the exception of Indonesia, all of these are, roughly speaking, NICs, with rapidly expanding industrial bases. Indonesia offers both oil and a strategic geopolitical position as valuable collateral. In 1967, the combined Gross Domestic Products of these dozen nations was $130 billion, equal to about 16 percent of the U.S. economy; by 1981, this was up to well over a trillion dollars, equal to 38 percent of the U.S. economy. Exports of the twelve debtors expanded even more rapidly, from $15 billion in 1967 to $190 billion in 1981, or from the equivalent of less than half of American merchandise exports to over four-fifths of them.[2]

The process was often controversial, for industrialization is no sociopolitical panacea. Military regimes often forced the march toward economic development and used political repression to manage indebted industrialization. The rapid expansion of modern industry and agriculture threw tens of millions of displaced peasants into swollen cities in search of jobs in the new factories. The teeming urban and rural poor reaped little benefit from national economic growth; in most countries, their well-being declined relative to the middle and upper classes. In some areas the poor may have become poorer in absolute terms.

Most LDC leaders and their bankers, however, were concerned with economic growth, not egalitarianism. From Algiers to Seoul, from Ankara to São Paulo, huge industrial complexes were created. Consumers in the developed West began buying Brazilian shoes and Korean shirts, and a few business travelers may have remarked upon the new Brazilian commuter airplanes they were riding. American steelmakers, long preoccupied with the Japanese threat, were caught unaware by cheap steel from Yugoslavia, Venezuela, Mexico, Brazil, Argentina, and South Korea. Automobile producers watched apprehensively as South Korea, Yugoslavia, Taiwan, Brazil, Malaysia, and other debtors developed modern automotive industries, began exporting cars, and threatened to follow in Japan's footsteps. The NICs had arrived, escorted by their bankers.

Brazil's foreign debt is the developing world's largest, and the Brazilian experience epitomizes the larger process. Brazil is the economic giant of the LDCs; its economy is larger than Canada's, nearly twice the size of India's, larger than the economy of Africa minus South Africa. Brazil is one of the world's great producers of steel, automobiles, textiles, and weapons, in addition to such primary products as coffee, sugar, orange juice, and soybeans. Its industry has attracted $25 billion in investment from foreign corporations, and São Paulo's 15 million-person metropolitan area is now the largest industrial center in the Western Hemisphere and perhaps the world. São Paulo and Rio de Janeiro, two hundred miles to the north, are frequent stops for the world's bankers, as Brazil's foreign debt is over $100 billion, and four-fifths of it is owed to international financiers.

Most of Brazil's foreign borrowing was managed from Rio de Janeiro, where in 1982 Marcilio.Marques Moreira, then vice-president of Unibanco, one of Brazil's banking giants, gave me a brief history of his country's borrowing experience: "Until the late 1950s and early 1960s, most of the foreign capital that came into Brazil was direct investment by foreign corporations. This began changing in the early 1960s, for both domestic political reasons and developments on international markets. Politically, foreign direct investment became more controversial. Especially after 1964 there was a shift towards loan capital." In that year a military coup overthrew the populist Goulart regime and installed a conservative military government. The authoritarian regime was generally friendly to multinational corporations, but it preferred its foreign capital in the form of loans that could be channeled to influential local businesspeople and bureaucrats.

Moreira continued: "In principle, the new government was ideologically favorable to foreign direct investment, but in practice it was especially oriented toward borrowing. By 1968, more and more private funds were coming in. Especially after the 1974 oil shock the public borrowers came onto the market, with very ambitious import-substituting schemes in energy, steel, petrochemicals, fertilizers, pulp and paper." Apart from Brazil's general desire to stimulate domestic industrial growth, the soaring cost of Brazil's oil imports spurred a new push to substitute domestic for imported goods.

"The state-owned companies," Marques Moreira continued, "have been the big borrowers. Eletrobrás, Petrobrás, CVRD, Siderbrás—with its component parts Cosipa, CSN, Usiminas, Tubarão—are all important debtors. Tubarão, by the way, is a joint venture with Kawasaki Steel, and the Kawasaki people say it will be the most modern steel mill in the world. Sunaman, a development bank for the shipbuilding industry; DNER, the national highway system; Telebrás; Nuclebrás. [This last is the national nuclear energy companies.] Even some companies owned by local states, like the São Paulo state electric energy firm."

Marques Moreira's list is well known to international bankers. For fifteen years, the so-called Bras brothers—Petrobrás, Eletrobrás, Telebrás, Nuclebrás, Siderbrás—were among the most frequent Euromarket borrowers. Eletrobrás, the electric energy holding company, owes over $8 billion abroad; it borrowed to build the world's two largest electric energy projects, Itaipu on the Brazil-Paraguay border and Tucuruí in the Amazon. Petrobrás borrowed over $7 billion to finance oil exploration and development as well as large petrochemical projects. The Siderbrás steel trust owes about $6 billion; telecommunications giant Telebrás, mining conglomerate CVRD, the railroad system, owe billions more. Government-owned banks borrowed abroad to re-lend to domestic companies. The national development bank, BNDES, which makes cheap long-term loans to Brazilian industrial corporations, used $3 billion from abroad and guaranteed another $4 billion in Brazilian borrowing.

Foreign banks provided investment finance for electric energy projects and petrochemical plants; a massive expansion of the country's steel mills, railroads, and telephone system; and huge iron and bauxite mines in the Amazon jungle. By 1981, the country's state industrial corporations accounted for over one-quarter of Brazil's investment and production and half of its foreign debt. Most of the rest of the public sector's debt was owed by government-owned banks like the BNDES and the Banco do Brasil.

Celso Martone, a leading economist at the University of São Paulo, describes how the Brazilian economy used foreign borrowing:

> Foreign financing was concentrated in three sectors. First was the capital goods industry, which consists primarily of private Brazilian firms and joint ventures between Brazilian and foreign enterprises. Second were the industries producing basic inputs: steel, petroleum, petrochemicals, fertilizers, aluminum. Third was the economic infrastructure: nuclear and electric energy, transportation (like the subways of São Paulo and Rio de Janeiro or the Ferrovia do Aço, a big railroad to the new iron mines), ports, communications.
>
> In all of these the state is of extreme importance. The last two groups are owned by the government, and the capital goods industry relies on heavy government stimuli. So the debt is, in effect, concentrated in the hands of the government. The idea was to develop Brazilian resources—research and development, technology, raw materials—and make Brazil a real world power by the end of the century.

Private Brazilian businesses also expanded phenomenally after 1967, and much of this growth was directly or indirectly debt driven. The growing state enterprises placed massive orders for machinery, equipment, and construction materials—intermediate and capital goods provided primarily by local private corporations. In addition to the bonanza of state orders, the Brazilian private sector got another bonanza of cheap financing. As the public sector grew, so did the network of private suppliers that fed it; so, too, did the myriad of foreign corporations that concentrated on supplying the automobiles, appliances, and other accoutrements of affluence demanded by the sprouting middle class of technicians, bureaucrats, managers, and skilled workers.

Brazilian industry matured rapidly. Between 1965 and 1980, Brazil's industrial production quadrupled, the size of its economy as a whole more than tripled, and the Gross Domestic Product per person doubled, all after accounting for inflation. The country now produces more steel and automobiles than Great Britain, and exports so much inexpensive steel that North American and European steel-makers are frantic about Brazilian competition. Brazilian private businesses, too, grew spectacularly, led by capital goods producers, the makers of heavy equipment used by other industries.

As the new debt-financed factories came on line, Brazil became a major exporter of manufactured goods. Total exports grew from barely $1.5 billion in 1965 to over $20 billion in 1980. The new exports were not just shoes and shirts. Former Planning Minister and investment banker João Paulo dos Reis Velloso noted in 1984, "a world-scale export offensive cannot be sustained just by traditional sectors such as textiles and footwear. It is necessary to play for even higher stakes, and to become competitive in other dynamic and technologically sophisticated sectors. This means, in Brazil's case, competitiveness in exporting basic inputs, capital goods, automobiles and trucks, engineering services and, as soon as possible, electronics."[3]

Exports of steel, chemicals, and engine blocks supplanted coffee and sugar, and in 1978 Brazil became primarily an exporter of manufactured products for the first time in its history. Embraer, the largest general-aviation manufacturing corporation outside the United States, has sold hundreds of small and medium-sized airplanes abroad to customers that include many American commuter airlines and Britain's Royal Air Force. Brazil is now the world's sixth-largest weapons supplier, with overseas arms sales of over a billion dollars a year. The huge Brazilian construction companies that grew along with industry—the three most profitable private Brazilian companies are in construction—took their skills abroad to build airports, steel mills, dams, highways, hotels, and shopping centers all over Latin America, Africa, and the Middle East.

South Korea also used foreign borrowing for industrial growth, and was exceptionally single-minded in its emphasis on exporting manufactured goods. In 1961, South Korea's income per person was only $87, equal to about one–thirty-third of the American average; today it is $2,000, about one-eighth of the American average. In the early 1960s, South Korean manufacturing accounted for barely one-eighth of the nation's total output, while today it accounts for a third, a proportion far higher than that of the United States. The Republic of Korea now has a foreign debt of nearly $60 billion, and this foreign capital has been crucial in rushing the country from abject poverty to industrialism.

As in Brazil, most Korean borrowing was done by government-owned banks and corporations. Utilities, transportation and communications, the steel industry, and especially the all-important public banks borrowed billions in the quest for rapid industrialization. Government access to foreign finance reinforced the Korean tendency toward extremely close government-business cooperation. Like Japan, which it resembles in many ways, South Korea came to be dominated by a few enormous industrial, financial, and trading conglomerates.

The dynamic Korean conglomerates are large by any standard. In 1985 the four biggest—Samsung, Hyundai, Lucky-Gold Star, and Daewoo—had combined sales of almost $50 billion, equal to almost two-thirds of Korean Gross Domestic Product economy. Samsung, with 1985 sales of nearly $16 billion, would rank twenty-third among American corporations, behind USX but ahead of GTE; Hyundai's $15 billion would place it twenty-sixth, behind Tenneco and ahead of United Technologies. Hyundai's shipyard in Ulsan is the world's largest such corporate facility, and its Changwon mill is the world's largest integrated machinery plant. The country's steel industry is one of the world's most efficient, and its shipbuilding industry is second in size only to Japan's.

Korean industrial growth relied heavily on overseas markets. The turn to exports dates back to the early 1960s, as Mahn Je Kim, president of the Korea Development Institute, explained in 1977: "Like many developing countries, Korea, until the early 1960s, followed an industrialization strategy based primarily on a policy of import substitution. In the early 1960s, however, after completing the relatively easy import substitution in nondurable consumer goods and their inputs, Korea changed its industrialization strategy from import substitution to export promotion. This new export-oriented strategy was first adopted by the military government that came to power in 1961, and was greatly strengthened by the exchange rate reform of 1964 and subsequent major policy reforms."

Results came rapidly, Mahn Je Kim recalled.

Korea's rapid economic growth actually began with the shift in industrialization strategy. Korean exports, which had averaged less than $25 million annually, increased very rapidly in the 1960s, particularly after 1962. Export expansion during 1962–76 averaged over 40 percent annually, rising in nominal value from some $55 million and 2 percent of GNP in 1962 to approximately $7.8 billion and 32 percent of GNP in 1976. . . .

In the 1950s and early 1960s, most Korean exports were primary products—tungsten, iron ore, fish, raw silk, agar-agar, rice, coal, etc.—while manufactured exports constituted only a small fraction of the total. After 1962, however, the latter expanded much more rapidly than the former. By 1976, manufactured goods such as clothing, electrical machinery, textile fabrics, iron and steel sheets, plywood, footwear and wigs, which had constituted only 27 percent of the nation's exports in 1962, had risen to almost 90 percent of the total.[4]

South Korea's export success was indeed stupendous. One-tenth of all the foreign finished steel the United States now buys comes from South Korea; Korean-brand appliances like Gold Star take up more and more American shelf space; and three of the country's big industrial conglomerates are selling nearly half a million cars in the American auto market— quite a feat for a country that produced only a few thousand cars in 1976. Some Korean exports are invisible, since in their fear of American protectionism the Koreans often sell through such established American firms as RCA and General Motors; Daewoo, for example, sells its LeMans through Pontiac. Yet American consumers have spent billions of dollars on Daewoo's Leading Edge personal computers, Samsung's VCRs, Lucky's television sets, and Hyundai's Excel subcompact cars.

Not all the major borrowers were as successful as South Korea and Brazil at accelerating their industrial growth, but the results were often impressive. Fifteen billion dollars in borrowing helped Mexico's oil monopoly, Pemex, find and develop rich oil deposits in the 1970s, along with new petrochemical and chemical plants. Mexican government borrowing also built steel mills, power stations, subway lines, and irrigation works, while private firms amassed $13 billion in debts to expand everything from machinery and auto parts factories to breweries. The Venezuelan government parlayed oil wealth and loans into huge new iron and bauxite mines, steel and aluminum mills, and other industrial projects in the Amazon; private firms used dollars for new industries and to give Caracas some world-class shopping malls and luxury condominiums. The Algerian desert bloomed with oil and debt-financed steel, chemical, and textile mills.

Foreign bankers made strange and varied allies around the world. They considered radical socialist Algeria a good risk, as one banker said, "because it's totalitarian and if the government says people will have to cut back consumption, they will."[5] At the other end of the political spectrum, foreign finance bankrolled the extreme *laissez-faire* policies of the Chilean military dictatorship. The nationalist Peruvian junta, right-wing South Korea, Marcos' Philippines, nonaligned Yugoslavia, and unsettled Argentina were all darlings of the international financial community.

Some of the uses to which borrowers put Euromarket money were undesirable by any social or economic yardstick. In Chile, much of the borrowing done by private firms and individuals went to fuel speculative booms in real estate and the stock market. In Zaire, Indonesia, and the Philippines, corrupt officials siphoned off large quantities of foreign funds. An unmeasurable portion—one estimate is one dollar in twelve—of all the money borrowed by developing countries went to buy military hardware.[6] And, of course, there was no assurance that debt-financed projects would be worthwhile. For example, Brazil's Nuclebrás spent billions of borrowed dollars to establish a nuclear power industry, much of which is now being dismantled as unnecessary and unsafe.

The most egregious misuse to which borrowed funds were put, undoubtedly, was capital flight. At different times in Argentina, Mexico, Venezuela, the Philippines, and other countries, the government borrowed dollars only to resell them in local currencies to investors who promptly redeposited the money in accounts in Miami or Zurich. This was especially common when the value of the local currency was artificially high in dollar terms. In January 1982, for example, the Mexican government was holding the peso at four U.S. cents, which most people thought was twice its real value. A wealthy Mexican with 25 million pesos could buy a million dollars with overvalued pesos, open a San Antonio account, and wait for the inevitable devaluation. Soon the peso was down to two cents and then to a penny; by January 1983, the million dollars was worth 100 million pesos, so that even after taking into account the 80 percent inflation rate, the smart speculator had more than doubled his money in a year. At the height of this insanity, in January 1982, Mexican capital flight averaged $30 million a day.

Although borrowers squandered countless billions on capital flight, corruption, and conspicuous consumption, they made enough important investments to give many debtor nations major productive facilities they would otherwise lack. Since the 1960s, the center of gravity of some of the world's more important manufacturing industries has shifted out of North America and Western Europe to the Newly Industrializing Countries of Latin America and eastern Asia. Low wages give the NICs obvious advantages in such labor-intensive industries as clothing, footwear, furniture, and consumer electronics; and they have developed surprising strength in such heavy industries as shipbuilding, steel, automobiles, chemicals, and petrochemicals. Even Japan can no longer compete with the NICs in major segments of the steel, shipbuilding, and automotive markets. Foreign loans have allowed many borrowers to increase industrial output and exports enough to both grow and service their debts.

The long-term economic effects of the international lending of the 1960s and 1970s were just becoming clear when the underpinnings of the arrangement began to erode. The success of the system depended on two factors. First, international markets for NIC exports needed to expand constantly if those countries were to service their debts. Second, interest rates had to remain reasonably low and predictable. In the early 1980s, NIC export markets dried up and the international interest rates to which their debt was tied soared.

In 1980, the industrial countries of Western Europe and North America descended into a period of economic stagnation and decline that lasted longer than any such recession since the 1930s. As industrial production dropped, unemployment rose; and as incomes declined in the industrialized nations, they bought less and less from the NICs. After thirty years of continuous growth averaging 10 or 15 percent a year, world trade stood still, and the NICs were especially hard hit. The recession also strengthened latent trade protectionism against some of the NICs' best trading hopes— steel, shoes, textiles, chemicals. Suddenly the dollars that the debtors needed to make interest and principal payments were drying up.

The borrowers were also hit by rising international interest rates. International bank loans are tied to the London Interbank Offering Rate for Eurodollars, or LIBOR; from below 11 percent in mid-1979, LIBOR went above 20 percent in early 1981. A country that had borrowed $10 billion at a floating rate of LIBOR plus 1 percent in 1978, when LIBOR was about 9 percent, had to pay under a billion dollars in interest in that year, about $1.3 billion in 1979, over $1.5 billion in 1980, and about $1.8 billion in 1981— even while the debtor found it harder and harder to earn dollars overseas because of depressed Western markets. Every time interest rates edged up 1 percent in the United

States and were transmitted to the Euromarkets, the big debtors were hit with another $3 or $4 billion in new interest charges. From 1978 to 1981, Brazil's net interest payments on its foreign debt went from $2.7 billion to $9.2 billion; in 1977, Latin America's debt service payments were less than a third of its exports, while by 1982 they were 59 percent.

The traumatic year of 1982 ended the latest round of LDC borrowing. Mexico was the first big debtor to go under. A combination of soaring international interest rates, the world recession, declining oil prices, and misguided policies drove the Mexican economy to the wall. By May of 1982, Mexico approached economic collapse. Lending ceased as the country's difficulties became evident, and in August, the country stopped payments on its bank debt. Fifteen years of financial optimism ended overnight. The smaller banks, who had come to the international arena in emulation of the international financial giants, were especially shocked to find that foreign lending was risky; they pulled out of the market almost immediately. When I visited a Pemex funding manager in September 1982, he showed me his empty anteroom in despair. "Six months ago," he said, "there were so many bankers in here you couldn't walk across the room. Now they don't even answer my telephone calls."

The banks practically stopped lending, and debtor dominoes fell all over Latin America. Bitter debtors recalled the sardonic Depression-era observation that foreign credit is like an umbrella lent in good weather, which has to be returned as soon as it starts to rain. New medium- and long-term bank loans to Latin America, according to the IMF, ran at about $2 billion a month through the first half of 1982, dropped to $1 billion a month in the last half, then to around $100 million a month in 1983 and 1984. To be sure, the banks lent over $13 billion to Latin America's besieged borrowers in 1983, but only as part of massive loan reschedulings and renegotiations that began in 1982; most of the loans made after 1982 simply went back to the banks to cover unpaid interest.

By 1983, new lending to the developing countries was at a standstill, apart from a few still-trusted borrowers in Asia. The debt crisis had become international. Thirty-four developing and socialist countries were renegotiating their bank debt; another dozen were in serious trouble. The problem list was led by fifteen countries in Latin America and the Caribbean with 90 percent of the region's people: Argentina, Bolivia, Brazil, Chile, Costa Rica, Dominican Republic, Ecuador, Guyana, Honduras, Jamaica, Mexico, Nicaragua, Peru, Uruguay, and Venezuela. Africa and the Middle East followed with fourteen reschedulings, most of them relatively small: Ivory Coast, Liberia, Madagascar, Malawi, Morocco, Mozambique, Nigeria, Senegal, Sierra Leone, Sudan, Togo, Turkey, Zaire, and Zambia. Only one Asian debtor, the Philippines, was renegotiating.[7] The most recent boom in international lending to developing nations was over.

The debt crisis moved relations between creditors and debtors from the marketplace to the political arena. As the various parties scurried to throw the burden of the crisis onto others, the battle over the debt crisis unfolded on two dimensions, one international and one domestic.

Internationally, debtors and creditors fought to extract as much as possible from each other. For the debtors, the stakes were clear: since no new loans were being made, their debts were nothing but a burden on their economies. In 1981, in fact, Latin America attracted over $20 billion more in foreign capital than it paid out in interest and profits to foreigners; by 1983, the continent was paying over $22 billion more to foreign banks and investors than it was receiving in new capital.

The day of reckoning had arrived: international bankers were no longer willing to finance their debtors' budget and trade deficits. Fifteen years of borrowing had exacerbated the problem: interest and principal payments were taking up huge proportions of government revenues and scarce foreign currencies. In order to meet the demands of their creditors, debtor governments needed to divert resources from pressing domestic uses to foreign banks. Debtor governments had to extract more resources from their societies by raising taxes, cutting back on spending, and increasing the price of government goods and services. Debtor countries also needed to increase foreign currency earnings to make debt service payments. This meant that workers had to accept lower wages to make exports more competitive, while local consumers had to consume less so that imports could be reduced.

The debtor governments, of course, attempted to avoid such politically unpopular policies, and to shift some of the adjustment costs onto their creditors. The bankers, these governments argued, could accept lower interest payments, wait a few more years for principal payments, and continue to lend until the crisis subsided. When bankers balked, debtors threatened to suspend payments or, more subtly, pleaded that the hardship needed to maintain debt service would cause unmanageable domestic political upheavals.

Creditors deprived of their contracted interest and principal payments, however, faced reduced profits and even bankruptcy. Banks wanted their money, and pushed the debtors to do what was necessary to get it. The international financial community, they argued, was simply forcing the debtors to undertake belt-tightening policies that were inevitable in any case. Since austerity programs had to be imposed, it made more sense to maintain cordial relations with creditors than to alienate them.

Jack Clark, Citibank's senior officer concerned with LDC debt, drew parallels for me between what international bankers felt the debtors needed to do and what the city of New York did during its fiscal crisis in the mid-1970s. New York City, like many LDC debtors, owed more to banks than it could manage to pay and was forced to cut back on spending and increase taxes. As Clark recalled in 1985, "What they've really got to do is what was done here in New York. Ten years ago this place was bankrupt; its credit standing went from substantial to zero almost overnight. Here, when they saw the problem, they were wise enough to cut back. You know, people were killed in the subways because there weren't any police down there, and that's terrible. Under the circumstances, the wiser thing would have been to see the problem earlier, but they didn't. That's what the developing countries should be saying now."

Creditors used powerful weapons to try to bring the debtors around. They pointed out that errant debtors might be frozen out of future borrowing for another thirty years. The banks could also threaten to seize whatever assets the debtors might hold abroad—an Aeromexico jet at O'Hare Airport, a Peruvian government bank account in London. Perhaps most ominous to the debtors was the banks' ability to cut off trade credits, the short-term lines of credit that are used in the everyday course of world trade. A country unable to use normal short-term credit lines would be forced to transact all its international trade on an unwieldy and perhaps impractical cash-and-carry or barter basis.

Jack Clark notes that the banks' bargaining weapons are strong but not all-powerful: "The banks try to create as many negative incentives as they can think of: they cut off trade credits, they stop financing government programs. I remember the Senegalese got in very bad shape, and we announced that we weren't going to finance their rice imports. That got their attention very quickly. That might result in a more positive environment. Beyond that, it gets hard. We talk a lot about attaching assets, but that's not really a strong weapon in most cases. Most of these countries don't have a lot of assets to attach. I remember we were going to do that with the Sudanese, and they said, 'If you can find anything we've got of value, go right ahead.' "

In addition to the difficulty in making credible threats against countries with little to lose, the creditors themselves faced a major problem of coordination. The very largest international banks, with long years of experience in and commitment to international operations, were ready to spend a great deal of time, energy, and money keeping their channels to debtors open, in the expectation of future business. But many of the smaller banks that came to international lending very late had little inclination to throw good money after bad, solely in the interests of supporting an international financial system they now wanted nothing to do with.

The first reaction of many small banks, especially from the United States, was simple: try to recover as much as possible, then get out. Mexico might not have enough overseas assets—Aeromexico jets, Pemex tankers, New York bank deposits—to satisfy the claims of a Citibank, but these assets certainly could cover the few million dollars in Mexican debts to a small bank in Ohio or North Carolina. The logical thing for the Ohio or North Carolina bank to do, then, was to attach Mexican assets as quickly as possible. Once this process started, of course, it would be impossible to stop a perverse bank run in reverse, as hundreds of creditor banks scrambled to get the debtors' few assets before each other.

The major international banks worked out an elaborate arrangement to reconcile the cross-cutting interests of hundreds of diverse banks. The pattern was set largely by a thirteen-bank advisory committee established to supervise the 1982–1983 rescheduling of $28 billion in Mexican debt owed to 1,400 foreign banks. Citibank's William Rhodes chaired the committee, which simultaneously carried out negotiations with the Mexican government and kept other banks informed and involved. Each of the six other American banks on the committee—Bank of America, Bankers Trust, Chase, Chemical, Manufacturers Hanover, and Morgan Guaranty—was responsible for liaison with ten more middle-sized banks in the United States, and each of these was in turn in touch with ten smaller American banks. The Bank of Montreal dealt with other Canadian banks, the Bank of Tokyo with Japanese and other Asian creditors. Four European institutions—Deutsche Bank, Lloyds, Société Générale, and the Swiss Bank Corporation—divided up responsibility for ties with other European bankers. Keeping smaller banks in line could involve as little as simple persuasion or as much as threats of large-bank retaliation in the interbank market. In some instances, the large banks were forced to buy the debt of small banks that simply refused to go along with the proceedings.

The most important forces for creditor cohesion, however, were the banks' home governments and the International Monetary Fund. It did not take long after the crisis began for economic policymakers around the world to realize that widespread LDC defaults would cause a wave of bank failures, with major domestic repercussions in every nation whose banks were involved. The United States, especially Federal Reserve chairman Paul Volcker, took the lead, despite the initial recalcitrance of more provincial members of the Reagan administration, such as Treasury Secretary Donald Regan. Volcker and his opposite numbers in other major central banks were directly involved in most of the debt renegotiations; the central bankers' Bank for International

Settlements extended billions of dollars in emergency bridg-
ing loans to major debtors. National authorities also pressured their own bankers to cooperate in the rescheduling
process; an insistent phone call from Paul Volcker to the
president of a small Michigan bank was usually enough to
keep the bank from bolting. In the interest of international
financial order, the central bankers sometimes prevailed on
all creditors, including the largest, to give debtors easier
terms than they would otherwise have done. In return,
regulatory authorities were usually willing to relax their
standards for evaluating the portfolios of banks involved in
major debt renegotiations.

The International Monetary Fund was at the apex of this
creditor pyramid. As overseer of the international monetary
and financial system, the IMF stood ready to organize, supervise, and enforce the necessary agreements. As debt
renegotiation followed debt renegotiation, by 1983 a standard pattern was set. When a debtor requested relief, the
banks made such relief contingent on an IMF stabilization
loan to the debtor. The debtor entered into negotiations
with the IMF, which demanded assurances that the debtor
government would cut budget deficits, reduce inflation, trim
wages, and reduce consumption. If the debtor agreed, the
IMF released a first installment of its loan, which served as
a signal to creditors that the debtor was going to undertake
the appropriate austerity measures. The international banks
followed with a private agreement, for example, to extend
principal payments for twenty-five instead of seven years
and to lend additional money. The IMF monitored the debtors, releasing new loan installments when performance was
good and witholding them when debtors failed to meet IMF
austerity targets.

Threats of defaults led the banks to make some concessions, especially in reducing interest-rate spreads and

lengthening the loan maturities (due dates). Counterthreats from the IMF and creditors kept most debtors from simply refusing to bargain. Incentives worked to similar effect, as the home governments of major banks stepped in to offer billions of dollars in short-term loans to help troubled debtors surmount immediate problems.

The American economic recovery after 1983 eased some of the suffering among debtor nations. Yet LDC debt did not go away; indeed, the restructurings and renegotiations only increased the debt burden in the long run in return for short-term relief. The cross-cutting interests of borrowers trying to rekindle economic growth and bankers trying to get repaid remain in conflict.

If the international dimension of the debt crisis was complex, its domestic dimension within the LDCs complicated matters still further. After 1983, conflict broke out in all debtor nations, as at the world level, over who would bear the burden of the inevitable adjustment. The costs of the economic austerity to keep up debt service were hardly welcome. Cuts in government budgets threw public employees out of work or reduced their salaries; they also forced the elimination of social programs. Policies to increase exports and reduce imports pushed wages and domestic consumption down; they also cut into business's profits.

As debtors spun down into industrial depressions more severe than those of the 1930s, massive layoffs swept Santiago, Mexico City, Manila, Seoul, and the metropolises of just about every other debtor nation. Political crisis was usually not far behind. Industrial workers, the middle classes, and local business people turned against the austerity needed to maintain good relations with overseas bankers and the International Monetary Fund. "IMF riots" swept Jamaica, Brazil, the Sudan, the Dominican Republic, and other borrowing governments besieged by their bankers and their people alike.

The crisis helped to solidify opposition to the Brazilian, Argentine, Uruguayan, and Peruvian governments, all of which eventually turned power over to civilians. The Marcos regime lost economic control, and political power followed soon after. Postcrisis Mexico was wracked by a newly powerful opposition, largely based in an outraged middle class and business community that saw its upward mobility frustrated by economic stagnation. The South Korean military's decision to tighten the country's collective belt with a vengeance led to unprecedented urban rebellions and eventually to the tense atmosphere in which President Park Chung Hee was shot by his own security chief in late 1979.

Brazil's domestic reflection of the debt crisis was especially dramatic. As Brazilian overseas interest payments soared, the government cut government spending, slashed wages, raised domestic interest rates, and induced an industrial depression. By 1982, virtually the entire country was calling for a new government. The poor were pushed even closer to starvation, and food riots swept the country's major cities. Throngs of impoverished street peddlers so crowded city sidewalks that municipal governments had to set aside whole squares and parks for the vendors. Industrial workers lashed out at government-mandated wage cuts, and strikes shook the nation. The government cut the budgets of the big state companies to free up money for debt service, and hundreds of thousands of government employees hit the streets to, according to their placards, "Defend the state enterprises and national sovereignty." Their leaders charged that "the government wants to turn the state enterprises over to international capital" and plaintive banners lined the streets of Rio: "The economic miracle went by, the party is over, and we weren't even invited."

Brazil's bitter business community became a hotbed of antigovernment feeling. In an interview late in 1984, Dilson Funaro, a leading São Paulo businessman, recalled the sorry picture: "The government needed to rebuild its credibility abroad and decided to adopt a monetarist policy here as bad as, or worse than, that of President Reagan in the United States. . . . That is, domestic interest rates would be brought into line with foreign interest rates which, in the United States, were reaching levels never seen in the history of capitalism. This was an extremely incompetent step. . . . It was a very violent shock. And from then on costs have exploded and it's been impossible to control inflation."

Albano Franco, president of a powerful group of private industrialists, the National Confederation of Industry, also criticized the government's apparent submission to foreign bankers: "The cure for Brazil's ills does not lie, temporarily or permanently, in the monetarist doctrine of international institutions that act as tools of domination of the rich nations and the multinational bankers. It is not Brazil's fate to work to pay interest, or to borrow to cover principal payments."[8]

Celso Martone, of the University of São Paulo, explained to me in 1983 why the Brazilian government's austerity program was meeting with such resistance from conservative industrialists: "The government had in the 1970s assured the capital goods producers of cheap finance and of a constant flow of orders from the big government projects. When austerity began and plans were cut, government orders got cut and interest rates rose. The capital goods sector was left with huge idle capacity. The sector stagnated, and it may even be in the process of liquidation. With all this idle capacity, there is a real possibility of technical backwardness as producers fall behind." By 1984, national production of capital goods had dropped to barely half that of 1980.

As the depression dragged on, the government lost whatever domestic legitimacy it had enjoyed. Many of the big projects decayed; the head of the country's largest private firm spoke disdainfully of "a veritable unfinished symphony of grandiose projects, all begun but none yet completed."[9] One of the country's leading humorists, Luis Fernando Verissimo, trained his guns on the government's desperate attempts to please foreign creditors. In one column he imagined the obsequious manager of the Banco do Brasil's New York branch telling two New York bank robbers that the bank was temporarily out of money: "If you gentlemen would care to come over to my desk, have a cup of coffee, I can explain. . . . Please, let us negotiate." Weeks later, the two hapless stickup men were still on a continual round of banquets thrown by the apologetic Brazilian authorities. "The main thing," the Brazilians told each other, "is not to arouse any suspicions."[10]

Dilson Funaro also charged the military government with indefensible incompetence in its conduct of the debt renegotiations: "From the very beginning the government placed itself in an unfavorable position: it negotiated at a time when the country had no reserves and had to submit itself to demands. The result was that the Brazilian populace was penalized far too much." The only remedy was for the government to step down. "At this point I think only a new government could restore our credibility and change the directions of the negotiations."[12]

As workers, slum-dwellers, the middle class, and the business community alike attacked the government, the military limped back to the barracks in ignominy. In February 1985, an unlikely alliance of business people, Communists, labor leaders, and the middle classes took power under the first civilian president since 1964. New debt renegotiations began immediately, and soon Dilson Funaro himself was running economic policy as finance minister. The crisis brought to the fore in Brazil, as it did in most other debtor countries, social and political leaders inclined to shift most of the adjustment burden onto the foreign banks.

Third World debt is not going to disappear as a major international and political issue. Concerted action by the IMF, national governments, and the major international banks can probably continue to avoid any truly catastrophic consequences of LDC debt-servicing problems for the international financial system. Yet major disturbances to the delicate structure of international debt would certainly affect the ultimate stability and viability of modern international banking. The debt crisis has already led many small and medium-sized banks to abandon international operations and return to more familiar domestic shores.

Most international bankers are, however, cautiously optimistic about the future of their relations with Third World debtors. John Heimann of Merrill Lynch believes that the whole crisis was overblown in the first place: "There was never a chance that LDC debt was going to topple the world banking system, because it was in no one's interest to have it happen—except maybe the press. All that was just editorials and third-rate academicians and headline hunters. But it was never going to happen because the system wasn't going to let it."

Jack Clark of Citibank recognizes that the halcyon days of the 1970s will not return to LDC lending, but looks forward to moderately favorable, if less frenzied, times. "I think just about every bank that's in the business feels that we overdid it, and for a very substantial period of time there will be very little additional lending. But this is a good business, and down the road it will start to pick up again. A lot of banks that today are saying they want to get out of international lending will be back five years from now, when economies get going and the debt is perceived to be much less of a problem."

Potential problems remain, for the simple reason that foreign debt is an enormous burden for a whole host of LDCs. Continuing difficulties in their domestic or international economic relations might lead some debtors to attempt relief at the expense of their creditors. Debtor governments must indeed consider whether the payoff for good financial behavior outweighs its pain.

The most direct problem foreign debt causes for developing countries is the sheer necessity to divert scarce domestic resources to international financiers. The average LDC is now paying about 5 percent of its Gross Domestic Product in interest and principal to overseas creditors; a comparable proportion of American output would be well over $200 billion, a sum equal to more than half of what Americans pay in federal income tax. For debtor governments to transfer such enormous quantities abroad they need to dramatically reduce government spending and increase taxes. By the same token, the LDCs need to earn foreign currency for debt service, which means they have to continue to cut imports and to expand their exports to the developed countries. This requires continued compression of wages and consumption; it also requires a constant battle against the Western protectionism that threatens to seal off the LDCs' most important markets.

In addition to the monetary cost of debt service payments, LDC debtors confront an international financial community that is increasingly insistent about the kinds of domestic policies it wants the developing countries to adopt. Before 1982, international bankers were generally willing to supply capital to any developing country that seemed successful, or even seemed as though it might be successful in the future. Bankers are now wary of unorthodox or interventionist economic policies, and want some sign of conformity to accepted financial principles before they reschedule existing loans or make new ones.

International bankers insist that borrowers abandon many past policies, especially those aimed at protecting the domestic market. The international financial community firmly believes in the marketplace as the best form of resource allocation, not a surprising attitude for financial institutions that are the arbiters of how financial resources are allocated on the world's capital markets. The idea is simple: intervention in the economy for social or political purposes ultimately reduces economic efficiency, slows economic growth, and erodes creditworthiness.

Jack Clark thus believes that the debtors have to adopt far more market-oriented policies than they have: "Not nearly enough attention is addressed to what these countries are doing to hurt themselves. They can't control protectionism or the high level of U.S. interest rates, but they can control things like domestic deficits, domestic inflation, money creation, exchange rates, import controls, whether the government enterprises are in everything."

Clark worries that the debtors have not adapted to changed international economic conditions with appropriate policies to increase their attractiveness to foreign investors:

> The developing countries had a lot of growth in the seventies; to some extent it was financed by the banks, and now we've turned off that tap. We provided capital for ten years, and they didn't even have to think about turning to their domestic resources and getting the very best out of them. The banks aren't there now, and the developing countries should be saying, "Well, we no longer have the bank credit, what are we going to do as an alternative?" The answer isn't to print a lot of money; the answer is to make much better decisions about allocating

domestic resources, and to do everything you can to attract capital from abroad.

They've really got to think seriously about how to bring in foreign investment, attract capital, and mobilize effectively the resources they have; and they aren't doing it. There's some progress. You hear talk about privatization in some countries. Mugabe in Zimbabwe has done a good job, and they're getting results; it's the only country in black Africa where the agricultural sector is growing, and it's growing because they've got a good incentive program. But those stories are few and far between.

I just spent a day with [Zambian President] Kenneth Kaunda in Lusaka, and he's a classic example. He said, "Mr. Clark, what you say is theoretically correct but socially unjust. We've got to have cheap food for our people." Well, his vision of social justice is ruining the country. My idea of social justice is to let producers get paid, and let consumers pay for what they consume. In real terms, and over the long run, that will work out. But the typical politician doesn't see that.

Countries that follow the policies preferred by international investors can hope to benefit by attracting new foreign capital, or by renegotiating existing loans at favorable rates. Good financial behavior can help keep lines of trade credit, and even export markets, open. Well-behaved debtors may also reap diplomatic and political rewards from grateful creditor governments. As an added bonus, the orthodox economic strategies prescribed by the International Monetary Fund and private international bankers may actually succeed in returning debtor economies to balance and setting the basis for future economic growth.

Nonetheless, the international financial community's economic prescriptions are open to theoretical and empirical questions. Even the purest of theorists recognize that markets often fail to produce optimal results, and admit scope for politics to affect the market mechanism. The question ultimately is not whether governments should manipulate economies, but when, how, and how much. Historically, in fact, all the currently industrialized countries pursued interventionist paths to economic development. Britain relied on predatory mercantilism and colonialism throughout the Industrial Revolution. The U.S. government was deeply involved in major public works in the nineteenth century, and had some of the world's highest tariff barriers until the 1930s. France, Germany, and Japan all relied on manipulated financial markets, trade protection, and direct and powerful government intervention in the economy during their industrialization drives. Some of these countries moved away from their chosen forms of state economic management after their industrial prowess was achieved and assured, but others maintained highly interventionist government policies or have returned to them in recent years.

In practice, the evidence that free-market economic policies produce good results in the Third World is spotty at best; the most serious followers of LDC *laissez-faire,* the Chilean and Argentine military governments of the 1970s, are generally regarded as economic failures. The two countries grew rapidly during a few boom years, then crashed disastrously in the early 1980s. Averaging out the boom and crash, Argentina's economy did not grow at all during the 1976–1984 military regime, while since 1973, Chile's economy has grown by a very unimpressive 2 percent a year. In contrast, the Brazilian military's highly interventionist economic policies produced an annual growth rate of over 6 percent between 1967 and 1984; South Korea's has averaged nearly 10 percent since 1965; and even Mexico, often cited as an example of the failure of LDC government interventionism, has grown 5 percent a year since 1965.

The most serious objections to the international bankers' economic orthodoxy in the debtor countries, however, are not theoretical but pragmatic. Powerful constituencies in every debtor nation depend on government support, whether it is theoretically defensible or not. Industrialists rely on tariff protection and government subsidies. Farmers clamor for cheap credit, workers for cheap food, the middle classes for well-paying government jobs. Even if the evidence were unambiguous that *laissez-faire* policies lead to greater social welfare in the long run, extraordinary domestic pressures make them virtually impossible to implement in most LDCs. If the maintenance of cordial ties with international financial markets demands the removal of government protection to important domestic groups, these groups will demand that such ties be severed before they allow themselves to be sacrificed.

Cordial relations with international financial markets may be worth their steep price, however, if international trade and payments are dynamic enough to actually make their long-term attractiveness outweigh the short-term cost of maintaining access to them. But if the world economy spirals downward, the good graces of the international bankers will be of little value. The more it looks as though ever-expanding exports and loans are things of the past, the greater the temptation will be for LDCs to confront their creditors head on.

Jack Clark indeed worries that continued economic stagnation in the LDCs may eventually exacerbate the debt crisis: "There are two sorts of adjustments. One is external, and there the developing countries have done fantastically well. Thank God they have, because it saved us. But on the internal side they're not doing well at all. They keep servicing the debt, but they don't get economic growth. When developing countries realize, five years down the road, that that's all that's happening, I'm worried that there will be kind of a reaction. If a big country—Argentina, Brazil, or

Mexico—tries it, all of the banking system's problems would suddenly re-emerge."

Ironically, one of the more serious potential causes of debtor frustration comes from within the developed countries themselves. Enough LDCs have been successful at using foreign capital to develop new industries, and at exporting industrial products, to worry business and labor leaders in North America, Western Europe, and Japan. Insistent pressure from Western producers in competition with LDC exports continually threatens to make it extremely difficult for the debtors to earn the foreign currency they need to service their debts. International bankers are thus fighting a battle on two fronts: one to keep their own markets open to the exports of their overseas clients, another to convince these clients that good financial conduct is in their own interests.

Since 1965, the international financial markets have become a sort of connective tissue between the industrialized economies and those of the Third World. For fifteen years international banks channeled Western savings and OPEC oil revenues toward the LDCs, and helped speed industrialization in the borrowing countries. Today both developed and developing nations confront the results of $600 billion in Third World bank debt.

Many of the debtor countries are now stiff competitors of industries in North America and Western Europe. American workers and owners in such labor-intensive manufacturing sectors as steel and garments are under continual pressure from the newly industrializing debtor nations. Yet a reduction in the sales of the debtors' products in the United States and other developed economies would exacerbate the debtors' difficulties, and thus weaken the global banking system. International financial instability could in turn seriously damage the interests of American international banks, and of their stockholders and depositors.

The resolution of the debt crisis will depend on the delicate balance between the international financial obligations of debtor governments and the domestic political pressures on them. This balance itself is contingent on a similar balance within creditor countries, between those concerned primarily with safeguarding the international financial system and those worried first and foremost about reducing foreign pressure on the domestic economy. In evaluating their alternatives and devising their strategies, the debtor governments will be guided by how the international economy itself grows, and how the policies of the industrialized countries respond to the evolution of the world economy.

6

The Future of International Finance

International banking is leading the world economy into a new era whose contours are unclear. Capital now moves across borders in such quantities and at such speed that the ability of national governments to formulate economic policy is seriously circumscribed. Investors, firms, and policymakers used to the comfortable familiarity of national economic conditions now compete for finance on a global capital market they cannot control or fully understand.

Global financial markets are changing the shape of the international economy. Debt-financed industrialization in the Third World is shifting the center of world industrial gravity from North America and Western Europe to Asia and Latin America. Financial markets are accelerating the evolution of the developed economies away from manufacturing and toward services. International currency markets that drive exchange rates up and down with a vengeance are causing major swings in the international competitiveness of whole national economies.

The world economy is entering uncharted waters. For hundreds of years, economic and political systems have been primarily national and coterminous; business people and workers have taken their economic grievances to national governments. No government responds for the actions of international financial markets, and national policies are increasingly powerless in the face of a truly global banking system. Nonetheless, while capital may be extraordinarily mobile, most people—and most businesses—cannot move from activity to activity, or from place to place, in response to marginal economic changes.

In every country with well-developed international economic relations, the dictates of global markets are in increasing conflict with the demands of firms, industries, and groups at the national level. International bankers, and many other economic actors around the world, have a vital interest in maintaining and deepening international financial and economic integration. Yet global markets threaten the livelihood of more insular business people and workers, who want to stop or even reverse international economic interdependence.

In the United States, as in the rest of the world, the country's international financial relations are deeply entangled in domestic politics. The United States is increasingly subject to developments on international capital and goods markets. For some, this financial openness is the source of enormous profit opportunities, and they do what is possible to reinforce and protect contemporary international financial integration. For others, the country's exposure to international competition is a disaster, and they fight to restrict economic integration. The resultant battles can pit industry against industry, region against region, workers against management, and eventually, perhaps, country against country.

The future of the international political economy, and of international finance, depends on how conflicting interests concerning the new economic realities are fought out in the political systems of the world's nations. The international political economy might move ever further toward economic and political integration, an outcome which would subject nations and peoples to the ever-increasing, and often unpleasant, discipline of international market forces. The world might divide into more self-contained and protected investment and trading alliances, which might undermine existing international political relations. Or international economic relations might stumble from problem to problem, raising the specter of uncertainty and even collapse.

The starting point for whatever direction the international political economy takes is today's highly integrated Western world economy. Robert Slighton, Chase Manhattan Bank's chief international economic forecaster, points out that strong and deep financial and trading ties bring together every capitalist nation: "The single broad trend of the postwar period has been increased economic interdependence. The proportion of world trade to world output has increased dramatically. Even more dramatic has been the increased interdependence of world capital markets, to the point where it is almost a misnomer to talk about a national capital market. There is a *global* capital market, period. The United States is just a part, although a very major part, of the global financial market."

The global capital market is in part a result of new technological developments that make it easy to move information and money from place to place. In Walter Wriston's words, "technology has combined with finance in a new and unique way that makes obsolete some of the old ideas of compartmentalized national markets."[1] Wriston's variant of technological determinism argues that ever more complex production methods, and transportation and communications advances, have forced businesses to expand their horizons ever further.

In this sense, contemporary international economic integration is simply part of a natural historical progression in which markets have grown in scale over time. Charles Meissner, of Chemical Bank's World Banking Group, who is a University of Wisconsin-trained economic historian, likes to take the long view: "Prior to the coming of the railroads in the United States you had very regional markets. To the extent that they were tied together, it was primarily by water traffic, either coastal or river. The railroads allowed us to assemble the factors of production on a national basis, and to market on a national basis. Beginning in the 1920s, and accelerating after World War II, came the organization of the world market. The development and blooming of the multinational corporation began to organize the factors of production on an *international* basis. The necessity for international capital arose, not only to support short-term trade and finance, which it had done for a long time, but for corporations themselves needing longer-term capital."

New technologies could only create a worldwide financial system, however, because political forces encouraged and tolerated them. Since World War II, the economic and political leaders of all Western nations have been generally committed to international economic integration. This commitment flowed from the widespread rejection of fascist economic nationalism, from the general belief that economic integration would increase prosperity and reduce social tensions, and from the sheer self-interest of important economic forces who found national markets limiting. An overarching concern, especially on the part of the United States, was to use economic relations among Western nations to cement their political alliance and weaken the hand of those who favored a neutral or pro-Soviet stance. In any case, policies to strengthen international economic interpenetration were relatively easy to adopt and implement through the early 1970s, for their effects were marginal, and in any case mostly positive.

Political consent made the global financial integration of the past thirty years possible, and political consent will be needed for this integration to advance. The most concerted political support for a continuation of current trends comes from the international business community. This includes both global banks and multinational industrial corporations with truly international production, distribution, and technological networks. International financial leaders and their allies around the world have battled to maintain international economic openness against the more insular pull of national politics.

International bankers have powerful and concentrated interests in a financially integrated world economy, since their business is central to such a world. The more international trade and investment increase without government interference, the more scope there is for private international financial institutions to extend trade credits, exchange currencies, take deposits, and make loans. The material interests and ideological tenets of the world's bankers lead them to insist that policymakers heed, not controvert, even untoward international market trends.

If economic internationalists prevail politically, and the postwar trend toward greater international economic integration is simply projected forward in a straight line, the result will be a capitalist world with truly global financial and goods markets and general political acceptance of market judgments. Walter Wriston believes that a fully integrated world economy immune from political interference is on the near horizon. "Today," Wriston has said, "except in a very few instances, national borders are no longer defensible against the invasion of knowledge, ideas, or financial data. . . . We now have a new calculus which, I believe, will in the end be beneficial to the world. It exerts global pressure on all governments to pursue sounder economic policies because it is becoming increasingly obvious that it is now impossible to hide in our new electronic world."[2]

Should the political influence of such market globalists as Walter Wriston be as strong as their preferences, the capitalist world will move toward economic integration free from political interference. In such a world, firms and individuals, labor unions, and politicians would all accept the verdict of international markets on the most efficient use of their time and energy. The economic role of government would be restricted to smoothing the transition of workers and capitalists from uncompetitive to competitive industries or regions, helping to organize markets, and providing a sympathetic judicial and social environment for private international transactions.

The organization of the world's businesses on a global basis will, in this view, allow the market to decide how resources can most effectively and profitably be mobilized. International banks and corporations are the leading edge of the new order, says Wriston: "The reality of the global marketplace has been the driving force pushing us along the path of developing a rational world economy. Progress that has been made owes almost nothing to political imagination. It has been the managers of the multinational corporations who have seen the world whole and moved to supply mankind's needs as efficiently as politics would allow."[3]

The attraction of market globalism is that it subjects all economic decisions to the scrutiny of international investors who can weigh potential profit opportunities around the world and encourage those that make the most economic sense. The argument is vaguely Social Darwinian: because economically impractical enterprises cannot survive in the long run, it is better that they never be started in the first place or, if they exist, that they be closed as quickly as possible. Globally integrated markets would not allow firms, workers, and governments to make costly mistakes—investing in unprofitable industries, acquiring unnecessary skills, adopting misguided policies. In the long run, increased economic efficiency improves living standards across the board; a rising tide, as the aphorism goes, lifts all ships.

Nevertheless, stubborn domestic groups and political leaders can erect important obstacles between national and international markets. They can impose trade barriers on imported goods or grant subsidies to exporters. They can prohibit firms from firing redundant workers or can enact policies that keep national wage levels higher than the market dictates. They can give tax breaks, government credit, and government contracts to businesses that would otherwise succumb to foreign competition for markets or capital.

Walter Wriston says impatiently, "As a general rule, the politicians have been engaged in fragmenting the world, while the multinational corporations have been viewing the planet as a single marketplace."[4] Wriston's dismay is echoed by policymakers restless about the recalcitrance of national governments to respond to this changing international reality. Anthony Solomon, then president of the Federal Reserve Bank of New York and second only to Paul Volcker among the U.S. government's financial decision makers, worried in 1982 that "the pronounced increase in interdependence we have seen has so far done little to dislodge deeply ingrained opinions. Instead, most governments, whether in the industrial countries or in the developing world, still cling to unrealistic notions of national autonomy. . . . It is an illusion that full national freedom of action exists in the kind of world we have, and it is wiser to be honest about that and let go of the illusion."[5]

Given the formidable obstacles to global economic integration, even the most fervent believers in the desirability and inevitability of the process recognize that it will hardly be smooth. What they hope and expect is that the trend is in the direction they desire. Walter Wriston told me, "As Thomas Jefferson once said, you are not transported to liberty on a featherbed. We're in a revolution right now, and it's being driven by technology. There is nothing the politicians can do—they can play King Canute for a minute, but the political process eventually catches up with technological innovation. That doesn't mean the halcyon days are here, or the wonders of world government, but I would argue that it's putting a closer noose in a shorter time frame on the political action of every country."

Increasing economic interdependence, Wriston believes, already so restricts the maneuvering room for national politics that it cannot be reversed. The economic attractiveness of every major nation, sector, and firm is being evaluated continually by thousands of bankers, traders, and investors around the world. Since government decisions affect profit opportunities, international currency markets pay close attention to political trends, and new policies are almost immediately reflected in currency values and capital flows.

The sheer size and speed of global financial markets makes them an economic force in their own right. As Wriston puts it, "The fact is that the foreign exchange market now amounts to around fifty trillion dollars a year and is just too big for any one entity to move. If you took all the capital of all the banks in the United States and sold it in the foreign exchange market, it would amount to about ten minutes of trading. The myth that somebody can influence a market of that size is just that."[6]

Many international bankers thus believe that the ability of international financial markets to move funds toward congenial political systems and away from hostile ones will eventually bring reality closer to their ideal world in which governments are unable to control them. As Walter Wriston said to me, "the political process has to be altered; the market-place will work in politics as it does in economics." He anticipates that politicians unable to attract capital to their jurisdictions will be turned out of office as their economies stagnate, and will eventually be replaced by leaders who can instill confidence in international investors. To an extent, predictions of global *laissez-faire* are wishful thinking, but they may not be any less accurate for that.

Governments all over the world are indeed under great international economic pressure. One type of pressure comes from the general international economic environment, which can be punishing to policymakers who ignore it; if domestic interest rates, for example, are held below international interest rates, capital will flow out of the country. Another type of pressure is more specific: the innumerable banks, firms, and farmers who have stakes in foreign markets, rely on foreign loans, or are tied to overseas suppliers and who push for policies to allow them to maintain access to world markets. The continuation and extension of postwar international economic integration depends largely on the ability of banks, firms, farmers, and employees with international interests to defeat their opponents in domestic political battle within the world's leading nations.

Whether or not economic interdependence leads to the most rational possible allocation of resources within and among nations, it certainly has costs that call forth political resistance. The maintenance of free goods and capital movements, for example, forces the gradual elimination of economic activities in one country that can be carried out more efficiently elsewhere. In an ideal interdependent world, the capital-rich and highly educated nations of North America and Western Europe would produce only goods that are intensive in capital and knowledge, concentrated in such sectors as high technology; labor-intensive manufacturing would be carried out in the labor-rich areas of the Third World. This may be rational and efficient, but it implies the extinction of tens of millions of jobs in the United States alone, and current jobholders cannot be sure that they would find employment in new lines of business. Politicians from America's industrial centers can hardly relish the prospect of the gradual demise of the industrial workers and industrialists they represent. True international economic integration radically reduces the room for independent action by governments to protect their constituents' jobs and living standards.[7]

For a large number of groups and industries, the rest of the world is an economic threat rather than an opportunity. Wriston's evolutionary faith in the inevitable triumph of a political environment favorable to economic openness, after all, relies on the assumption that, in the long run, popular pressures for economic growth will defeat bad policies; but most political pressures are for short-term protection from adversity rather than for abstract promises of long-term prosperity. Steel and automobile producers in North America, local business people and workers in debtor nations, and unemployed industrial workers in Western Europe may sincerely believe in international economic cooperation, but they also want to safeguard their immediate material interests, and thus desperately want to make national borders less open to international economic competition.

The impact of international financial affairs on domestic economics and politics is often unwelcome. Firms, groups, and politicians in industrial societies have thus tried to restrict the scope of international economic forces. Pressure for trade protection has mounted steadily in the United States since 1970, reaching its highest level during the early 1980s. Many European firms have turned away from volatile international markets toward more predictable bilateral contracts with customers in Eastern Europe and the Soviet Union; Western European politicians of all political views aggressively promote Eastern bloc trade. Traditional European industries have been vociferous in their demands for national, or Common Market, support against foreign competition. In Great Britain, the troubled industrialists' protectionism is mirrored by the economic policy positions of the left wing of the Labour party. The Labour Left, which represents about a third of the party, has over the course of the 1980s developed an Alternative Economic Strategy that calls for trade barriers, restrictions on international capital movements, and currency controls.

Broad coalitions in debtor nations are highly critical of their countries' treatment by international financial markets. Most of the Third World has in fact retreated from the general enthusiasm about global financial relations that was easy to muster while these relations were bringing capital in; now that bills have to be paid and capital is flowing out, international bankers are blamed rather than courted.

Serious international economic distress would reinforce the insistence of domestic forces that economic policy in the world's major nations look primarily inward. If the United States, Western Europe, Japan, and the major developing countries moved dramatically away from economic integration, modern international finance would almost certainly and automatically follow. Global banking grew in a postwar economic and political environment congenial to cross-border flows of goods and capital. If that environment changed in major ways—such as toward the formation of exclusive regional trading and currency blocs—global banking would fracture along with the rest of the world economy.

There is at least one discouraging historical precedent to today's international economic interpenetration. After the defeat of Napoleon, for over seventy-five years the United Kingdom dominated the international economy much as the United States did after World War II. International finance and trade centered on London, British free trade and overseas investments tied the world economy together, and the British Navy kept the seas safe for commerce. Many of the world's nations were drawn tightly into the international economy. Over time, however, new challengers to Britain's industrial lead arose: Germany, France, Japan, the United States, among others. From the 1890s on, more and more new centers of influence expanded their trade and investment, and eventually conflict broke out among some of them.

Contemporaries noted in the years before World War I, as they do today, that the world's major economies were increasingly interdependent. Yet the response of many economic actors to increased international integration was to demand vigorous government support. This helped feed increasing trade protectionism and even colonial annexation. The experience ended with two world wars, and ever since, scholars have argued about whether nineteenth-century economic interdependence fed or calmed international political and military conflict.

International financial leaders and policymakers are indeed well aware of the political threats to the continued health and growth of international financial markets. For Henry Wallich—who before his 1986 retirement was the governor of the Federal Reserve Board usually regarded as the board's international expert—the traumatic lessons of the 1930s reinforce his concern. Wallich, whose international financial experience goes back fifty years, draws upon history for current lessons about the need for "a world financial climate conducive to the free flow of capital. The history of the interwar and early postwar period tells us that this free flow of capital can by no means be taken for granted. A continuing effort is needed to preserve it. . . . From an international point of view, what most matters is to preserve the good functioning of the system. What we have most to fear is a return to a condition such as the 1930's, when the world froze over financially."[8]

Historical and current evidence of the stumbling blocks on the path to perfect international markets leads many observers, and even some bankers, to expect governments to intervene more, not less, in international economic affairs. After all, the result of the Third World debt crisis was to draw governments in both debtor and creditor nations ever more directly into international financial negotiations, and into domestic measures to cushion the impact of the crisis. Indeed, some of those most obedient to international market signals during the early 1980s, such as Ferdinand Marcos and the Brazilian military, discovered to their dismay that the domestic political costs were very high. Where economic interdependence harms domestic groups enough, it can create a backlash that demands increased political manipulation of international economic relations.

In the early 1970s, in fact, international financial leaders began noticing a disturbing trend away from economic internationalism in many national political systems, including the United States. American sentiment for trade protection grew, the Nixon administration abandoned the Bretton Woods monetary system in 1971, and many of Nixon's cabinet members showed little interest in international economic cooperation.

In 1975, Henry Kaufman, a senior partner of the important investment bank Salomon Brothers and one of Wall Street's most respected leaders, expressed concern about the political difficulties facing international business leaders. "Nationalism is on the rise again," Kaufman wrote. The implications were serious. "Unless we can arrest the rise of extreme nationalism, the multinational corporation will no longer be a growing force in international markets. Accelerating nationalism will mean increasing conflict between the economic rationality of the multinational corporation and the objectives of the sovereign state."[9]

At the same time, Paul Volcker expressed similar fears to an interviewer from *Euromoney,* the principal magazine of the international financial markets. Volcker, then a senior fellow at Princeton and a former Treasury under secretary, was within a few years appointed chairman of the Board of Governors of the Federal Reserve System, America's central bank; he was thus one of the two or three most powerful economic policymakers in the world. Volcker was concerned about the political future of the world economy: "Power is more fragmented; the United States can't play the same role that it did in the earlier post-war period. . . . My experience in recent years has made me very conscious of the difficulty of getting a cohesive co-ordinated policy when there is this much dispersal of basic power centers and a kind of self-consciousness of separate political and economic identities that goes with the dispersal. It increases the danger in my mind that one country or another, running into economic adversity, is going to adopt fairly self-serving policies, and these policies aren't going to help anybody in the long run."[10]

The difficulties of obtaining international economic cooperation lead Charles Meissner to observe skeptically, "For two decades we've been talking about economic interdependence and the necessity to manage interdependence, and we've done almost nothing about it." Since the early 1970s countries have, for example, found imaginative ways to restrict trade without officially raising tariffs. The United States has coerced dozens of countries to reduce "voluntarily" their American sales of cars, steel, clothing, shoes, and other products. The French have routed shipments of Japanese VCRs through an understaffed and remote facility in Poitiers, which seriously delayed their delivery. By 1985, American subsidies to agricultural exports were equal to about one-quarter of their total value, while Common Market agricultural export subsidies were about one-tenth of the value of its farm exports. Many countries have manipulated their currency and capital markets to protect domestic producers, and have worked out preferential agreements with selected customers and suppliers.

Governments are indeed hard put to resist pressure for policies that benefit their constituents at the expense of foreigners, especially if the only drawback is a vague assertion of the long-term undesirability of economic nationalism. The Chase Manhattan Bank's Robert Slighton thus told me that he thinks major steps toward international economic cooperation are unlikely: "We seem to be as far away as we ever were from agreeing as nation-states that we really need to cede a certain degree of policy sovereignty. To make policy on a cooperative basis we have to do things we really don't want to, but we're not very close to that. Now, the consequences of that inability to cede some degree of sovereignty, to build some sort of policy coordination, are the events we have seen over the past ten years. Barring a very unexpected and sudden increase in the willingness of countries to make policy on a coordinated basis, I think a significant reduction in the freedom of the trade regime is inevitable."

Should political pressure from domestic economic groups and sectors opposed to market globalism reach extremes, a cataclysmic breakdown of international economic cooperation might create the world of Walter Wriston's nightmares. Such a world would probably be carved into a few large semiexclusive economic blocs. The prospect, once more, conjures up dire historical images. When the Depression of the 1930s strengthened domestic demands for insulation from a hostile international economic environment, the world's leading economies simultaneously turned inward and looked for a few preferred economic allies. France and Great Britain raised economic walls around their colonial empires and redoubled their imperial economic activities. Japan quickened its construction of an East Asian Co-Prosperity Sphere that, at its highest point during World War II, stretched from Manchuria to New Guinea and from Burma to the Marshall Islands. The Nazis and their allies in southern and eastern Europe created a continental economy centered on Germany. The United States rapidly became the dominant economic power in the Western Hemisphere. As empires were sealed and continents closed off, economic competition fed diplomatic conflict and, eventually, war.

The doleful interwar experience notwithstanding, economic blocs might be a relatively peaceful way of defusing international economic conflict. After all, their purpose is simply to exclude competing and include complementary economies, and there are enough underdeveloped countries with cheap labor and raw materials to go around, so to speak. Indeed, formal and informal measures have already gone quite a way toward creating three broad economic alliances. The European Community now includes most of Western Europe; eight of its members' currencies are linked in the European Monetary System (EMS) so that they move up and down together against other currencies. The community has preferential economic relations both with nonmember countries in the Mediterranean basin and with the socialist countries of Eastern Europe. Most of the former African, Asian, and Caribbean colonies of the Common Market's members are tied to the community in an economic and financial-aid accord known as the Lomé Convention. At the same time, the United States has since 1980 moved toward preferential trade and investment ties with Canada, Mexico, and most of the nations in and around the Caribbean basin. For their part, the Japanese are once again building a strong position in the economies of East and Southeast Asia.

The economic uncertainty of the 1980s has indeed accentuated international economic coalition-building. Chemical Bank's Charles Meissner believes the process is fairly far along: "The EMS in essence is becoming a Deutsche mark currency bloc, and eventually the Brits are going to join as the British economy becomes more and more dependent on the European Community. You have the European Community as a Deutsche mark-driven system, then the dollar system—including especially Canada, Mexico, and Brazil—and probably the development of a yen system in the Far East."

Although a division of the non-Communist world into economic blocs might be a practical intermediate solution to the contradiction between international and domestic forces, interbloc relations might be less than harmonious. Meissner says that he is "very scared" of the possibility of "the development of three common markets and a breakdown in the trading system. The Europeans build special bilateral relationships with Africa, primarily for raw material and energy access. The community in essence turns inward and forms a self-sufficient common market tied to resource and energy bases abroad. They force the United States to do the same in the Western Hemisphere, and the Japanese to do their own bit. Or perhaps you get the Community on one side and a very large common market in the Pacific basin."

Meissner worries that competing economic alliances are already pulling at the political cohesion of the Western world. "You can see all of the flags going up in Europe; the Europeans are well on the way to isolating themselves already. You can see it in legislation in the United States on the free trade area with Canada, the development of our special relationships with ASEAN [the Association of South East Asian Nations], greater U.S.-Japanese cooperation in the Pacific, the opening of China to both Japan and the United States. All the seeds are there. Rather than a unified market-oriented international system, there would be in essence a trilateral economic system based on three economic and currency groupings. This would reinforce neutrality in Europe and neutrality in Japan, with the United States more isolated from its allies. It would be destabilizing in the long run."

If the world economy stagnates or spirals downward into depression, the incentives for individual nations to disassociate themselves from global markets may become so enticing as to lead to a resurgence of economic nationalism. Challenges may arise from nations passed by or pushed downward by international economic trends, or by social groups and classes within nations similarly deprived by the reigning economic order. The decay of the system could feed itself. The more defections there are from the existing international economic order, the weaker is the mortar that holds that order together.

The principal political weakness in the delicate political structure of international financial integration is, ironically, also its principal source of strength: the United States. America's commitment to international economic affairs is constantly open to question. The very size and natural resources of the United States makes economic autarky more feasible for the United States than for any other capitalist nation. If, for whatever reason, the United States decided to withdraw from its economic commitments to Europe and Japan and to re-concentrate its forces in the Western Hemisphere, the effects would be far more devastating to the rest of the world than they would be to the United States itself. By the same token, social and political forces sympathetic to economic nationalism are much stronger in the United States than in most other advanced industrial nations; no other country has such powerful real and potential lobbies for economic insulation. Larger segments of the American business community remain domestic in orientation than in any other industrial nation, whether they are in retail trade, real estate, construction, local manufacturing, or military contracts.

In the early 1980s, the deepest recession since the 1930s rekindled traditional American misgivings about the international economy. Some of the country's most important firms reeled under foreign competition. Massive layoffs devastated the industrial Midwest. Business people and politicians spoke openly of the need for new economic policies to save the country's traditional manufacturing industries. Perhaps most dramatically, the farm community was torn apart by a homegrown debt crisis. Like many developing countries, American farmers borrowed heavily in the 1970s to invest in new land and machinery, for they expected a continuation of rising farm prices and of interest rates barely above the rate of inflation. After 1980, when interest rates rose and prices fell, farmers across the country had to meet doubled or tripled interest payments with shrinking sales. Between 1980 and 1986, farm prices dropped 20 percent while the cost of farming rose 15 percent. The farmers, like the debtor countries, worked harder to get by. Still, farm income dropped precipitously in the 1980s to one-half its 1970s levels as from 1980 to 1986 the number of family farmers fell by one-quarter. Thus farmers, like the LDC debtors, turned to the political battlefield for relief; foreign competition and the banking system were popular targets. The farmers' fury was shared by many workers and business people in the steel, auto, lumber, electronics, machine tools, and clothing industries.

In the midst of economic hardship in America's heartland, the country's international financial relations came under fire. Populist farmers and import-competing business people alike attacked the big-city bankers who had lent tens of billions of dollars so that other countries could undercut American producers. As the Third World debt crisis unfolded, many Americans looked disapprovingly at the billions extended to Third World debtors and their creditors by governments in North America and Western Europe. It was, after all, difficult to understand why the U.S. government let American farmers go broke but bailed out the Argentine government. As California Congressman Jerry Lewis said in blasting government loans to Brazil at the height of the debt crisis: "It would indeed come as a surprise to most people that the deficit-ridden Treasury had cash to spare for short-term loans (at interest close to the T-bill rate) to say, American timber mill or steel plant operators who suffer from similar problems and who would appreciate a Treasury as solicitous of them as it is of their Brazilian counterparts."[11]

An important demonstration of how domestic economic distress in the United States might affect the international financial system came at the height of the debt crisis. In 1983, the Reagan administration asked the U.S. Congress to approve an $8.4 billion increase in the U.S. contribution to the International Monetary Fund. The international financial community regarded strengthening the IMF as essential, while many domestic political forces in the United States opposed the use of taxpayers' money to strengthen a system they did not support.

The battle over the U.S. quota increase became the most hotly contested and closely fought struggle over American foreign economic policy since the 1940s. It pitted the world's leading private bankers and business people, and the combined weight of the Reagan administration, against domestic American political forces with little sympathy for international financial integration. The extraordinary difficulty the IMF's supporters had in the United States is an indication of how hard it may be to reconcile national politics with the needs of global capital markets.

The International Monetary Fund plays a central role in international finance; former president of the the New York Fed Anthony Solomon has called it "the best friend that market-oriented people have in the world we live in."[12] The debt crisis that began in 1982 gave this international financial police officer more to do than ever before. By 1983, dozens of countries—compared to one or two in the normal year—were in different stages of IMF programs designed to enforce good financial behavior. The fund had made so many stabilization loans that it was in danger of running out of cash. The IMF's available funds had to be increased; since these funds are met by quotas from member nations, each member had to increase its contribution. Agreement was eventually reached on an approximately 50 percent increase. In most countries, national legislatures—where they were even consulted—quickly passed the necessary bills.

In the United States, opposition to an $8.4 billion additional American contribution to the IMF arose almost immediately. The international financial community looked on aghast at the possibility that provincial Congressmen might bring international financial markets to a standstill. Jacques de Larosiere, managing director of the IMF, voiced widespread fears that failure to increase the fund's resources "would cripple this institution" and have "incalculable consequences for economic and financial stability worldwide."[13]

The Banker's Association for Foreign Trade (BAFT) coordinated and led much of the bank lobbying for passage of the IMF bill. This sixty-five-year-old lobbying group describes itself as "the leading spokesman for the international banking community." The Washington-based organization, with about 135 American banks as full members and another hundred foreign banks as nonvoting members, is a concentrated and specialized political organ of the American international banks.

Washington lawyer Gary Welsh was centrally involved in the IMF quota conflict; he worked for BAFT during the legislative struggle. Welsh knows well both the principal obstacles to financial internationalization and the reasons for the bill's eventual passage. "There's a strong political resistance to the internationalization of our economy," he told me two years after the quota debate. "We got the fringes of the political spectrum against us. The Left was against it because they said it was taking money out of Social Security, and the IMF was making people suffer; they don't like big banks anyway. The Right was against it, too. They said there shouldn't be any of these organizations. We got caught in the middle. We found the Right much more dangerous in the debate; proportionally more Democrats in the House voted for the IMF than Republicans."

Politicians' positions on the quota increase, Welsh noted, reflected the international economic positions of their constituents. "States like Massachusetts and California are generally very supportive, because they have industries that are dependent on foreign markets, and they've moved away from industries that have been hurt by imports. Generally, the Southeast and the West are very difficult areas. So are big pockets of the industrial belt—places like Pennsylvania, Michigan, and Ohio that have been hit particularly hard."

The strange political lineup drew the labor movement,

the New Right, and import-competing industrialists together as critics of the banks and the IMF. Conservative Caucus chairman Howard Phillip lashed out at "government of the banks, by the banks, and for the banks" and Richard Viguerie, the Right's propaganda wizard, launched his biggest direct-mail campaign since the Panama Canal treaties. Reagan administration support for the bill aroused strong dissent among Republicans.

Both the labor movement and management in traditional industries regarded the measure as a giveaway to job- and plant-exporting banks and corporations. Henry Schechter of the AFL-CIO complained to Congress of "foreign loans that represented high risks, decreasing the supply and raising the cost of capital for domestic investment." William Hoppe, of Bethlehem Steel and the American Iron and Steel Institute, pointed out that the steel industry had lost over $3 billion the previous year, largely due to foreign competition. Hoppe reminded Congressmen of the proliferation in developing countries of "world-class sophisticated mills financed by foreign loans and directed to serve world markets," and presented figures showing that five major debtors—Argentina, Brazil, Mexico, South Korea, and Venezuela, with a total 1982 debt of $274 billion—had tripled their steel production between 1970 and 1981, while that of the rest of the non-Communist world rose just 3 percent. The steel industry representative concluded, "All this has the effect of translating part of an international financial problem into a steel overcapacity problem," and insisted that "the financial institutions of the world should not be made whole at the expense of an already troubled steel industry in the United States."[14]

Most of the protestors were primarily interested in using the debate as a symbolic opportunity to raise long-standing concerns over U.S. government support for international banking; few had strong feelings about the quota increase itself. Even so, as Gary Welsh recalls, "the bill was only approved because of some classic legislative deal-making. Garn and St. Germain [Jake Garn, a Utah senator and chairman of the Senate Banking Committee, and Fernand St. Germain, a Rhode Island congressman and head of the House counterpart] combined the IMF bill, which probably would not have passed the House on its own, with a whole series of bills on housing, community development, and a half dozen other things."

With few public supporters in their battle for the bill, the bankers had to rely on a behind-the-scenes network in the executive and legislative branches. "In the international area," Welsh says, "a very small club carries the stuff through Congress, and you've got to be in good communications, working together." Welsh lists the principal supporters activated during the debate. "The Fed, obviously, was crucial. Volcker saw the implications of everything much sooner than the Treasury did. We worked very closely with the Fed, particularly in responding to initiatives that came out of the Congress about regulating the banks. There were a lot of attempts in the course of the IMF bill to put restrictions on international lending by U.S. banks. We would need to come back, particularly through Volcker, and say they were a bad idea. Sometimes you don't want the banks to say it; you want the regulators to say it. There are ways to make your views known, and generally we'd talk to the Treasury, to the Fed, to the Comptroller [the Office of the Comptroller of the Currency, a Treasury agency that regulates many banks] and tell them the problems we saw. Then they would get up and testify, and say they had problems with this or that. So we had a very close working relationship with those three agencies."

Welsh points out that some members of the Reagan administration did not originally support the banks' position, but were forced by events to take a stand for the IMF quota increase:

> The Treasury Department only came around to being an ally after the Mexican crisis. Before the Mexican crisis, Treasury was questioning the need for IMF resources. There really was a lot of hostility there to international organizations. [Donald] Regan was essentially a domestic market guy, [Beryl] Sprinkel was very much a doctrinaire conservative, and [Richard] MacNamar really had no international experience.[15] It was only after the Mexican crisis that they came on board and started pushing the Congress. In fact, in some of the early hearings, people like St. Germain and Garn were asking, "Weren't you guys just telling us six months ago that we didn't need any money for the IMF, that it was not a wise use of our resources, that it was against Administration policy?"
>
> Eventually we worked closely with the Treasury; the permanent staff—the people who had always worked there—was very supportive. It was a matter of bringing the leaders along. The banks themselves became very close to MacNamar. They had a lot of meetings with him, and he became almost, in a sense, a spokesman for some of the major banks on the need for IMF resources.

In their attempt to rally support for the IMF quota increase, bankers tied the bill in with everything from international economic stability to the dire consequences for American national security if Latin American debtors staggered from financial crisis to revolution. James Robinson III, chairman of American Express—one of the country's major international financial powerhouses, even though it is not a bank—drew graphic connections between financial leadership and unrest south of the border. "It's been labeled a bank bailout bill," Robinson complained to a *Fortune* reporter. "The small-town politician or bank in Maine says, 'It serves those bastards right.' I'd like to ask how many able-bodied men between the ages of eighteen and twenty-four they have in their community and what size boots they wear. I'd tell them to get ready to go to Latin America, because you let some of those governments go populist and you're going to have national security problems."[16] Some of the bill's supporters pointed out that the $8.4 billion quota increase was technically a loan to the IMF and could be borrowed back at any time. Other IMF supporters argued that refusal to increase the quota would ultimately cost the United States far more than $8 billion in financial instability.

Despite the best efforts of the bankers' allies in the executive branch, by the time the bill reached Congress it was already so politicized that chances for its approval were considered slim. Only backroom deals and the assistance of Fernand St. Germain allowed the banks and their supporters to guide the bill through the House, where antibank sentiment was concentrated. Early on, the Administration and the bankers convinced St. Germain to support the bill, but he insisted that he needed to take a public position hostile to the financial community in order to maintain his political reputation and defuse opposition.

Welsh describes the process by which St. Germain shepherded the quota increase through the House in private, while attacking international financiers in public: "In the House Banking Committee there was a delicate balancing act. St. Germain said, 'Okay, I understand what's at stake here, but I know the House. I know that we're only going to sell it to the members of the House if we can convince them that we're beating you guys over the head.' We were totally dependent on him to get it through the House, because he was the chairman of the committee. And because he is such a vocal critic of the banks, a lot of people believe him. So St. Germain played a critical role in dealing with the popular political sentiment for punishing the banks; he had to convince people that it was being done."

Indeed, St. Germain was a major bank critic during the

debate. He opened one day of his committee's hearings on the bill, for example, with reference to "the deep concern that the international situation is, indeed, fragile and that the United States must ignore all else and ride quickly to the rescue. U.S. banks, trapped in their international adventures, have used this genuine concern to direct attention from their failings.

"U.S. banks have ignored prudent practices and domestic needs," St. Germain continued, "in search of the quick buck and sky-high interest rates offered by desperate borrowers caught in an international financial squeeze. . . . It ill behooves the Congress, the administration, financial regulators, or journalists to paper over banking excesses with flag-waving statements about the glories of financial colonialism."[17]

Even while he engaged in some politically prudent bank-bashing, St. Germain assured the bankers that the bill would go through. He also promised that a variety of restrictive amendments approved in the House version would be jettisoned in the joint House-Senate conference committee. As Welsh recalls, "The bills that came out of the House were terrible from an international banking standpoint. To get the IMF thing through St. Germain had to say, 'Banks won't be able to do this, they won't be able to do that; we're going to make them put up big reserves on all international loans.' It was a conscious strategy on his part to get it through the House. He'd tell us, 'Once we get in conference, I'll throw out all this stuff.' " The objectionable restrictions on international banking were indeed removed in conference committee once the bill passed the House.

Although American international bankers eventually got the IMF funding they wanted, the battle was extraordinarily protracted and difficult. Gary Welsh summarizes the lessons of the IMF debate for the political future of American international bankers: "What the bankers found out from the IMF process was that they weren't popular, which they always thought they were, and that there was a tremendous misunderstanding of what international lending was all about. The banks learned a tremendous lesson from that: they had done a bad job of communicating with their representatives and senators. We're now trying to build a whole system to disseminate information. We can equip our bankers with material they can go to their community with about the internationalization of the economy, about how we're dependent upon export markets, how imports play an increasingly important and beneficial role in many sectors of our economy, and how banks are a crucial element in financing these flows."

The bankers' interests conflict with those of many opponents with political clout, and public relations will not eliminate the fundamental disagreement. Welsh concludes that American international bankers will have to rely on their ties with strategically placed policymakers: "The banks have realized that they don't really have any independent political support in the Congress. Banks can't be up front on the issues; they've got to work very closely with the executive branch. The only way you can get this stuff through is with a strong administration, strong support from the Fed, and strong support from a dozen or so key legislators in Congress—the chairmen of the Senate and House Banking Committees, Foreign Relations Committees, the Speaker, people like that. You have to depend on the leadership to carry it through, so that's what everybody's working on."

The bankers' harrowing experience of very nearly losing the IMF battle demonstrates that the continued internationalization of financial and goods markets cannot be taken for granted. The IMF quota increase was a relatively small matter that only international bankers and some policymakers felt strongly about. The bill's opponents regarded it primarily as a symbol of overseas economic commitments that irritated them. Even so, the bill would certainly have lost without intensive administration lobbying and skillful work by the bankers' allies in Congress. Should the American political system be faced with the need to make a major and costly, not a symbolic, commitment to global market integration, there is little question that global markets would lose to traditional economic insularity.

If firms, investors, and workers in most of the world's nations were given a direct choice between the familiar, if limited, security of domestic markets and the unpredictable, if potentially great, opportunities of market globalism, the well-known would win over the unknown. For this reason, most international financial leaders are content to avoid posing such a stark choice. Because they know how difficult it is to obtain political agreement on national exposure to the international economy, many international bankers are willing to see current settlements simply limp along from sheer inertia. The existing patchwork of monetary and trade accords, investment treaties, and aid packages can hold if governments muddle through problems and crises. Much as they might hope that Walter Wriston is right about the inevitable triumph of one world market, most participants in and observers of international financial markets expect no more than that current political and institutional indefinition will evolve gradually toward greater international economic cooperation and will avoid serious shocks along the way.

Robert Pringle of the Group of Thirty, the New York-based international financial think tank, assumes that, over time, assaults on the open trading system and on the freedom of capital flows will be beaten back. Pringle says, "I don't see a breakdown in the trading system happening because the mutual stake in it is so high. If a basically open trading system does survive, I think it will be very hard to stop the developing countries from continuing to move ahead at a much faster rate than developed countries. Notwithstanding endless debates, the basic adjustments will go on, and this growth will be financed somehow. Banks will go on lending, and other capital market instruments will expand to meet those developing countries that have good policies. And enough developing countries will follow good policies to convince the capital markets that they offer good prospects of a real return on one's money."

Even if trade restrictions grow, international financial integration could probably continue. Cross-border capital movements can, in fact, take the place of international trade. A firm kept out of a market by tariffs can simply jump trade barriers and invest in the protected economy. Indeed, many American multinational corporations did this in the Common Market in the 1950s and 1960s, and many Japanese companies are doing so in the United States today. The process could be indirect, through the banking system: Japanese banks that would normally finance the investments of export-oriented manufacturers in Japan might, with the imposition of trade restrictions in the American market, simply shift to financing production within the United States.

The sheer technical difficulty of restricting financial flows might make them safe from all but the most extensive intervention. Robert Slighton of the Chase Manhattan Bank is indeed pessimistic about the future of international trade, but cautiously optimistic that trade problems will not impede international economic integration in the long run.

> I think the biggest headlines on the horizon are going to be about trade protection. I think a significant reduction in the freedom of the trade regime is inevitable. Some people argue that restrictions on capital mobility are also inevitable. There may very well be some attempts to restrict capital mobility, but it's virtually impossible to do so. You'd have to destroy a whole

set of markets and do a degree of policing that's hard to believe. I don't think efforts to restrict capital movement will be terribly successful. In terms of projections, I would first see trade restrictions that are reasonably successful in that they will tend to accomplish what they set out to accomplish—to restrict trade. Then, attempts to restrict capital mobility, which are not successful. Finally, perhaps some willingness to cede policy sovereignty, in the sense of agreeing to make policy on a coordinated basis.

As long as the world's leading economic powers are not openly hostile to international banking, the international financial system can continue to operate. In fact, John Heimann of Merrill Lynch points out that the global banking system has become expert in "adjusting itself for an unknown future, concentrating on trying to protect itself against the whims and fancies of governments." Heimann is sanguine about the ability of international finance to adapt to most government policies. "The sensibility of markets en masse is amazing. Financial systems can clearly adjust to anything; all they need is time. That doesn't mean that banks aren't going to go broke, and of course governments can interfere, but the system as a whole is going to work, assuming that reason always prevails."

Despite the myriad domestic pressures they face, financial policymakers have, Heimann believes, been quite successful at maintaining "ever-increased levels of cooperation in spite of the chauvinistic or nationalistic tendencies of governments. An awful lot of strides have been made in the right direction—most of them behind the scenes. But political pressures can always make things more difficult. Since we are dealing with mainly democratic nations and you can't have a dictatorship, political pressures are a reality. We just have to figure out how we are going to muddle through and hope that reason does prevail."

From the standpoint of the world's international monetary policymakers, too, there appear to be enough shared interests among the world's leading economies that working solutions can be arrived at. Problems are continually arising, and there is cause for concern—but not alarm. A high-ranking Federal Reserve official pointed out to me both the relative successes and the weaknesses of current arrangements: "As shown by the debt crisis, when there is a real problem, countries are prepared to see an institution like the IMF take on a bigger role. But it's hard to see any giant leap forward."

International bankers and international financial policymakers, then, share a background belief that the most that can be hoped for is low-level crisis management. As the Fed official said, "I think we're doing pretty well, given the fact that we don't have a supranational central bank that runs things. Looked at another way, I think most countries are operating in a fairly responsible way internationally. I guess I take some comfort from the fact that we're doing as well as we are, given the fact that there's no world government."

Although it is tempting to expect future international financial relations to evolve gradually and uneventfully, important tensions have been building in the international economy over the past fifteen years. Major changes are underway in the structure of the world economy, and in the structure of the domestic economies of most nations. Rapid industrialization in parts of the Third World have put great pressure on manufacturing industries in the developed countries, and the decline of manufacturing employment in North America and Western Europe has major social and political implications. At the same time, the interconnection of global financial markets has seriously restricted the ability of national policymakers to insulate their constituents from international economic events. The combination of structural economic changes and impotent politicians might well be volatile. If the dictates of global markets are distasteful enough to people in enough countries to create a virulent reaction against international markets, international banking would be an early casualty.

The call and response of international and domestic politics and economics will determine the future of international finance. Where on the continuum from autarky to globalism the world economy heads depends most directly on how well it performs. Substantial international economic growth gives countries, and the groups within them, incentives to tie themselves to world markets. A full-scale international economic crisis, however, would almost certainly push the world's leading economies toward some form of economic blocs; and the more serious the crisis, the more hostile the blocs will become. If the world economy neither returns to the extraordinary growth of the 1950s and 1960s nor disintegrates into a repetition of the 1930s, markets and politics will struggle through with a mix of conflict and cooperation.

Problems in international financial markets can fuel political pressures against economic integration, while political pressures can create international financial difficulties. Indeed, the prospect of a vicious downward spiral most alarms international bankers and financial policymakers. The precedent of the Depression is often invoked: the original crash provoked a round of economic nationalism, which prolonged and deepened the crisis, which in turn provoked a new round of international economic conflict, and so on. The analysis and the parallels are rough at best—analysts still disagree on whether trade and currency wars prolonged and deepened the Depression, and comparisons between the 1930s and the 1980s are unreliable—but the stakes are high enough for international financial leaders to worry.

How American politics responds to international economic developments is unquestionably the single most important determinant of the future of the world economy and of international financial markets. Although the U.S. economy no longer dominates international markets to the extent that it did in the 1950s, it is still far and away the world's largest. Three-quarters of all international financial transactions are in dollars, and the sheer size of the American economy and of its financial markets allows American trends to drive the offshore markets. No other country can single-handedly affect international interest rates, trade policies, and financial flows to the degree the United States can.

In the United States as elsewhere, international economic integration has brought great prosperity to many groups, regions, firms, and individuals, but it has also imposed limits on them and on others. If the benefits of prosperity outweigh the cost of the associated limits, and if the prosperous prevail over the limited, the world's economic and political systems will grow more intertwined. If, however, the pain inflicted by international markets surpasses the gain they might offer, the postwar economic order could disintegrate. The future depends on the attractiveness of international markets and on the political power of their supporters. The most decisive battles will be fought within the United States.

7

Invested Interests and American Politics

The United States is more sensitive today to international economic conditions than it has been at any time since the Civil War. Loans to the Third World threaten the profits of major American banks, while foreigners are crucial lenders to the U.S. government itself. American banks and corporations have a trillion dollars at stake overseas, and many of the country's leading firms depend on continuing international economic openness.

Powerful economic interests are invested in this new international political economy. American international banks are foremost among those with a self-interested concern for continued international economic integration. The country's major financial institutions are now inextricably linked to economic activities in other countries. Their global investments make them vehement defenders of economic interdependence.

At the same time, foreign competition for goods and capital is eroding the position of other American firms, and *their* continued survival may depend on *reducing* international economic openness. Foreign competition is the principal concern of many American manufacturers and farmers, and goods produced with low foreign wages hound American industrial workers. The result has been sustained pressure for government policies that restrict international economic integration in order to protect American businesses, jobs, or wage levels.

The internationalization of financial and goods markets since World War II is changing American politics and economics. International economic trends are straining the country's political system, while government policies are constrained by forces on international financial and currency markets. However the United States reacts to its international economic exposure, the outcome will determine the contours of American society and the international political economy, and with them the future of American international finance.

Most Americans are made aware of the increasing economic openness of the United States by the origin of the goods they buy. Consumers in the United States looking for electronic equipment—stereos, pocket calculators, television sets, radios, videocassette recorders, personal computers, tape players—are hard put to buy American. Foreign-made clothing, shoes, furniture, and housewares have captured large segments of the U.S. market, as have imported machine tools, steel, chemicals, and copper. Americans buy one-quarter of their cars from foreign companies, and many of the components used to assemble allegedly American automobiles are actually manufactured elsewhere.

American foreign trade has indeed grown dramatically. In the early 1950s, the United States imported goods and services worth less than one-twentieth of its Gross National Product, about $70 billion in today's dollars. In the 1980s, imports have averaged one-eighth of GNP, over $400 billion a year. In 1950, the average American consumed less than $400 worth of imported goods, expressed in today's dollars;

in 1986, the average American consumed more than $2,000 in imported merchandise.

While foreign firms have been expanding their exports to the United States, foreign corporations have been moving massively into the country. Foreign investors control American affiliates worth over $800 billion, and they own firms ranging from Carnation to United Press International. One American worker in twenty-five works for a foreign affiliate; in manufacturing, the figure is one in fourteen.

The foreign interests of American businesses are also extremely important. More than one-fifth of what U.S. industry produces is exported, along with two-fifths of the country's farm output. One-third of U.S. corporate profits are made in foreign trade and investments.

The country's openness to trade is very visible, but the exposure of the United States to international financial markets is broader and deeper. One-quarter of all the loans made by American commercial banks are made abroad; one-fifth of all the commercial bank lending in the United States is handled by foreign-owned banks. The country's twenty largest banks, which effectively direct the American financial system, do nearly half their business abroad. American nonfinancial corporations have come to rely on offshore markets for much of their borrowing. The federal government owes foreigners $300 billion, and pays about $25 billion a year in interest to foreign creditors.

The United States is part of an international financial system made up of a swirling mass of trillions of dollars, which can move from place to place at a moment's notice in response to economic and political events. Financial institutions in the United States closely track international interest rates and currency values, and major institutional, corporate, and private investors are important buyers and sellers of international financial assets. Indeed, the volume of

American international financial transactions is many times as large as its international trade. Offshore financial markets in the United States, the International Banking Facilities exempt from normal American financial regulations, now amount to over $300 billion.

International financial markets continually assess the economic attractiveness and political reliability of the United States, just as they do of Indonesia or Norway. For American companies to borrow on the world's lowest cost and fastest capital market, they must match the terms and conditions offered by firms and governments all over the world. The United States thus faces an international financial discipline similar to that faced by the developing-country borrowers, although the sheer size of the U.S. economy gives it great influence. If the United States satisfies the international financial community's economic and political requirements, it can have virtually unlimited access to enormous quantities of capital, and access to capital is the key to maintaining competitiveness in the global economy; if the United States falls out of international financial favor, it will lose capital and have to pay more for it.

The ability of capital to move rapidly from country to country and from currency to currency can put a tight rein on government actions. As early as 1969, Andrew Brimmer, a member of the Federal Reserve's Board of Governors, complained that the Euromarket had "greatly complicated—and made more difficult—the management of monetary policy in the United States." More generally, Brimmer noted, "in only a few years, this market has evolved into a mechanism capable of exerting a powerful external influence on domestic financial markets."[1] National policymakers must constantly consider the probable international financial reaction to their decisions. Even words must be carefully chosen, for the international markets are so sensitive to rumor and expectation that a statement by a senior Federal Reserve official can drive the U.S. dollar up or down in half an hour.

A high-ranking Federal Reserve official is indeed pessimistic about the ability of American policy to withstand international pressures: "We've had a growth in capital markets and capital flows which is really exponential. And it just gets bigger and bigger and bigger. In a sense, we've become a little country, subject to the same limitations as those countries face. The world's becoming more integrated puts limitations on what everyone can do; I guess we're *all* becoming small countries."

International financial markets can easily subvert the intent of a national government's domestic economic policies. In an economy closed to international capital movements, for example, policymakers might reduce domestic interest rates to stimulate economic growth; lower interest rates make it easier for firms and consumers to borrow to expand production and consumption. But in a financially integrated world, banks and other investors compare interest rates in all countries. Lower interest rates in one nation lead lenders to take their money elsewhere. Instead of reducing the cost of borrowing, then, government policies to reduce domestic interest rates might lead to an outflow of capital which would make it *harder* for firms and consumers to borrow. This chain of events plagued many developing countries in the early 1980s, as well as France in 1981, during the early months of a new socialist government.

Government spending plans can also be blindsided by international financial trends. If a financially closed national economy is in recession, the government can stimulate demand by deficit spending—borrowing to spend on public works or incentives to invest or consume. Because the economy is stagnant and profits are low, savers in this closed economy are willing to invest in government bonds. But in what economists call "an international world," the national government's bonds are in competition with investment opportunities all over the world, rather than just inside the country, which can force the government to pay dearly to borrow. Many LDC debtor governments learned this lesson to their dismay, when international banks turned off the tap of financial resources to them in 1982. Their governments' own investing classes would lend to them only at exorbitant interest rates. For example, Mexican and Venezuelan coupon-clippers would hardly accept lower rates of return on bonds of their governments than they could earn in the Miami money market.

Of course, global capital markets can work in favor of government policies the markets trust. If politicians who want to spend beyond the government's means can draw on the goodwill of international bankers, the resources at their disposal can be increased enormously. Attractive government policies can draw international finance toward them just as surely as unappealing policies can drive capital away.

In the late 1970s and 1980s, Americans got a taste of how trends in international financial markets could affect the U.S. economy. The Carter and Reagan administrations were torn between domestic demands for economic growth and the need to maintain the confidence of international financial markets. Their delicate balancing act led to extraordinary results.

After his election in 1976, Jimmy Carter tried to infuse life into a stagnant American economy. Growth ensued, but it was accompanied by a moderate increase in inflation. As the economy expanded and domestic prices rose, the United States sucked in imports. The merchandise trade balance went from a $9 billion surplus in 1975 to a $34 billion deficit in 1979. At the same time, capital flooded out of the United

States at the rate of $60 billion a year. Between 1976 and 1981, American banks increased their overseas claims from $80 billion to $300 billion, while American multinational corporations increased their overseas investments from $140 billion to $230 billion. As dollars left the United States to pay for imports or foreign investments, and as international currency markets reacted unfavorably to Carter's policies, the dollar dropped precipitously in value.

Between 1976 and 1979, the American currency fell by more than a third against the Deutsche mark and the Japanese yen. American banks and corporations with major international investments lost ground to their overseas competitors, as the dollar's value shrank and Wall Street worried seriously about inflation. Carter tried to keep the dollar from falling, but the international markets continued to bid up European and Japanese currencies.

In 1979, the Carter administration moved decisively to reduce inflation and strengthen the dollar. Government social spending was scaled down and Paul Volcker, the new head of the Federal Reserve, pushed interest rates up dramatically. The results of the Fed's new monetarism were quick: the dollar's slide stopped and inflation began to decline. But as the Fed drove the federal funds rate from under 8 percent in 1978 to 19 percent in early 1981, the economy spun into a deep recession in 1980 that helped lose Carter the presidency.

The Reagan administration supported Volcker's anti-inflationary monetarism and further reduced social spending. A second recession ensued, deeper than the first; between 1979 and 1982, American manufacturing production dropped 9 percent and median family income dropped 10 percent. Yet inflation was dramatically reduced, as the Consumer Price Index went from over 13 percent in 1979 to 4 percent in 1982.

As monetarism drove interest rates up and inflation down, militarism brought government spending to new heights. A dramatic increase in military spending began under Carter, and from 1978 to 1986, federal military expenditures almost tripled—they went from 4.8 to 6.6 percent of the Gross National Product, an unprecedented one-third peacetime jump. Because of soaring interest rates and heavy government borrowing, the government's net interest payments more than doubled as a share of GNP, passing $135 billion in 1986. All other federal spending declined as a proportion of GNP.

Monetarism and militarism produced extremely high American interest rates and a great demand for funds on the part of the federal government. Had global capital markets been wary of the Reagan administration, disastrous difficulties in government borrowing might have resulted. As it happened, however, the American government's anti-inflation resolve and pro-business policies impressed international investors. As both American interest rates and confidence in the United States rose—assisted by the debt crisis, which made the American economy look safe by comparison—money flowed back toward dollars and the United States.

The Reagan administration capitalized on its international economic reputation to finance soaring military spending and a widening budget deficit by borrowing hundreds of billions of dollars from abroad. Capital poured into the United States at the rate of over $100 billion a year after 1980; total foreign private investment in the United States went from under $200 billion in 1978 to a trillion dollars in 1986. The foreign demand for American assets increased international demand for dollars, and after 1981 the dollar shot back up against other major currencies, regained much of the ground it had lost under Carter, and kept rising.

The strong dollar of the early 1980s led Americans to buy more and more foreign goods, because the more expensive dollar made goods from abroad cheaper in dollar terms. The resulting import surge devastated firms and industries unable to compete with foreign producers. In the early 1980s, then, heavy government borrowing drew capital into the United States, which increased international demand for dollars; this raised the dollar's value and reduced the competitiveness of American goods in the United States market; hundreds of billions of dollars worth of imported products filled American shelves.

By 1985, the government's budget deficit was $200 billion, the country's trade deficit was $125 billion, and international financial markets began to worry whether the process was sustainable. The dollar slid again and a new round began.

By now it is clear to most Americans who follow the domestic economy carefully that there are strong connections between the country's international financial relations and domestic economic developments. It is widely understood, for example, that a lack of foreign confidence in the U.S. dollar makes American investments less attractive to international investors, and can force interest rates in the United States to rise as the American government and private firms scramble to borrow. The stock, bond, commodities, and money markets in the United States are extraordinarily sensitive to changes in financial flows into or out of the United States, and to changes in the value of the U.S. dollar. Often important market changes take place on the basis of expectations alone: the simple fact that in 1985 Congress passed measures to cut the budget deficit in the future was enough to reduce interest rates, since investors expected less future government borrowing, and thus to bring the value of the dollar down. When, in September 1985, financial authorities from the United States, Japan, West Germany, France, and the United Kingdom publicly encouraged the dollar to fall, currency traders reacted to the announcement by selling dollars massively, and the dollar dropped by 5 percent in a day.

America's recent international financial relations have left the United States with a legacy of policy problems for the early 1990s not unlike those confronted by LDC debtors in the early 1980s. In the 1980s, the United States government financed its budget deficit by borrowing heavily from foreigners, which raised the dollar's value, increased imports, and reduced exports. The country's subsequent trade deficit was paid for by a more general inflow of foreign capital.

Foreign lenders to the United States government will eventually want their debts repaid, and foreign investors in the United States will eventually want to repatriate their American earnings. At this point the country will face a familiar dilemma: the government will have to raise money to repay its foreign creditors, and the country will have to increase exports to offset the profits and interest payments foreigners will take home. Some speculative figures illustrate the point. By the end of 1986, the federal government owed foreigners nearly $300 billion, and foreign investments in the United States were over $200 billion more than American investments abroad. A reasonable projection would be that by 1992 the federal government will owe foreigners $500 billion in today's dollars, and net foreign investment in the United States will similarly be about $500 billion. At this point, assuming a 10 percent rate of return on the foreigners' money, the U.S. government will be paying about $50 billion a year in interest payments to foreigners, and the nation as a whole will need to export $50 billion a year more than it imports in order to offset the interest and profits paid to foreigners on their American investments.

The country's eventual need to service its foreign debt will require measures similar to those taken by other international debtors. As Federal Reserve governor Robert Heller puts it, "The game plan is thereby clear: reduce the growth in federal spending and substitute exports as the new driving force of the American economy."[2] Consumption and wages must be restrained in order for the United States to compete effectively and earn enough to repay its creditors. Of course, the comparison with the LDCs should not be overdrawn. American foreign debt is equal to only a tiny fraction of its annual GNP, while the debts of many LDCs are larger than their GNPs; and the United States, unlike South Korea and Brazil, can repay its creditors in its own currency. Nonetheless, the United States is now very much subject to international financial forces.

If the United States is now just another "small country" for the world financial markets, the American banking system is now just one part of a global financial order. The major American international banks are far less important internationally than they once were; only four of the world's twenty largest banks are American (nine are Japanese, four French, two British, and one German). As the United States has been drawn into the international financial system, American banks have come to compete for deposits directly or indirectly with the international financial markets. The inevitable result, American financial leaders believe, will be what the Fed's Robert Heller calls "a comprehensive overhaul of the entire financial system." Heller argues, "It has become abundantly clear that our financial system must be overhauled to bring it up to the standard that will be required if we are to remain the leading financial power of the world in the coming years."[3]

International competition has indeed forced the American financial system to change as much over the last fifteen years as it had in the previous hundred. Barriers to interstate banking have fallen, distinctions between banks and other financial institutions have eroded, interest rates have been decontrolled, and dozens of new forms of savings and lending have developed. According to Robert Pringle of the Group of Thirty, "countries are simply being forced, if they want to participate in this financial revolution at all, to adjust their practices accordingly. Obviously the American financial system has got to change, and it will change." This realization has indeed made an impression on American policymakers. Congressman Charles Schumer (Democrat–New York), who is on the House Banking Committee, supports interstate banking on the grounds that "interstate banking makes sense because in a world market, state lines don't make sense." Schumer similarly argues that controls on American interest rates are bound to fail: "If we put a ceiling on rates of money, then money will flow to Japan or Germany."[4]

If financial integration continues at its current pace, American banking will be remade to facilitate the transmission of market signals between international financial markets and the U.S. economy. A hundred or so major banks will be left at the apex of the market, all with important international operations and truly national networks. Several thousand local banks will concentrate on small-scale consumer business. The line will blur between commercial and investment banking, and between banks and other financial institutions; stocks, bonds, futures, options, and consumer credit will all be distributed by large financial conglomerates. The strength of the dollar and the level of international interest rates will become central pieces of economic information, and the international financial position of the United States will motivate much of the U.S. government's economic policy.

The sensitivity of the United States to the international economy constrains firms, politicians, and workers in striking ways, but these short-term constraints are not the most controversial consequence of international financial integration. Indeed, if the problem were simply one of learning how to design government, corporate, or labor policies in a more limiting international environment, the difficulties might be largely technical. The country's policymakers, business people, and labor leaders would need only to coordinate a concerted response to international economic events.

There are, however, major differences in interest and opinion about how the country's international economic relations should evolve. Economic openness is working broad and deep changes in the structure of the American economy itself. The costs and benefits of this structural change have fallen very unevenly on different industries, regions, and classes in the United States; they have enriched some and impoverished others. The changing nature of the American economy has thrown the victims and benefactors of the process into heated political battle, much of which centers on whether the country should deepen or fundamentally revise its international economic relations.

Political struggles that are barely beginning will determine how the United States responds to the world economy. Two intersecting and overlapping battle lines are being drawn. One is horizontal; it divides entire sectors of the economy on the basis of whether they are internationally competitive or not. Firms, workers, and regions besieged by foreign competitors for markets or capital seek assistance, such as trade protection and capital controls; those that do well in global competition fight against any measures that might endanger international economic openness. The second division is vertical; it is organized more on class lines, and pits those pulled up by structural economic change against those pushed down. Inasmuch as structural economic change increases income disparities, the country will become more politically polarized over the degree to which government should intervene to redistribute income. The groups relatively disadvantaged by social change will demand government support, while the advantaged will oppose political attacks on their income.

Those who can compete in the changing world and national economy press for economic internationalism and for market-oriented policies at home and abroad. The constituencies for this pressure, broadly speaking, include both firms and educated technicians and professionals in high-technology industries, finance, and such affiliated sectors as insurance and real estate, trade, and many services. Those whose ability to compete has eroded, on the other hand, demand government support. These forces include both management and labor in labor-intensive manufacturing, basic industry, and most of agriculture.

In a world where capital and goods move freely, indeed, the United States simply cannot compete with the developing countries in any industry in which the cost of unskilled or semiskilled labor is a major factor. Investors have no reason to back a textile mill in the United States when an identical factory in Taiwan or Brazil can be set up and operated at a fraction of the cost, especially when some of its output can be shipped back to the United States. As international trade and finance have grown, the center of industrial dynamism has thus shifted away from North America and Western Europe to the Newly Industrializing Countries (NIC).

Since 1960, the production of heavy manufactured goods has doubled in the United States, while it has almost quintupled in the developing world. Industry has become an increasingly small portion of the U.S. economy. In 1950, corporate profits in manufacturing were nearly three times as large as profits in the financial and commercial sectors; today, financial and commercial profits are greater than those made in manufacturing. Since 1950, manufacturing employment has dropped from 36 percent to 21 percent of the labor force. In 1950, for every ten workers in American goods-producing industries—manufacturing, mining, and construction—there were fourteen in service-producing industries; today, there are thirty service workers for every ten industrial workers.

Changing international production patterns have gradually made many American industries all but obsolete. Since 1970, the domestic clothing, furniture, leather, footwear, iron and steel, machine tools, radio and television equipment, electrical components, and motor vehicles industries have lost substantial portions of their sales and employment to foreign competitors. Mass-market videocassette recorders and compact disc players, both based largely on American technology and driven by American demand, are not even made by companies in the United States. The ledger is not all negative, of course; producers of high-technology machinery and equipment, aircraft, plastics, and tobacco have all gained substantially from foreign sales. The losers are nonetheless striking, for many are traditional mainstays of the U.S. economy. The result has been a split between sectors of the economy that are successful in global competition and those that are not.

The American automobile industry has lost much of its home market. Few of the automobiles sold in the United States are truly made in America. About one-quarter are produced abroad and sold by foreign companies in the United States; another sixth are made by foreign firms but sold under the name of the three American automakers; and almost a third of all the parts used in building cars in the United States are imported. In addition, factories owned by foreign firms—Honda, Nissan, and Volkswagen—produce more than 5 percent of the cars made in America. By 1990, Hyundai, Mazda, Mitsubishi, and Toyota will also have North

American factories, and American production by these foreign firms will be over 10 percent of the total market. The American motor vehicles industry, for most of this century the centerpiece of the American economy, has all but lost its international edge.

The three big American auto companies have responded in a number of ways. They have accelerated the shift of a great deal of their production out of the United States, while dramatically scaling back the size and wages of their American labor force. Half of their employees are now overseas, and since 1970 about half a million American jobs in the automotive and allied industries have been eliminated. Chrysler now gets well over half the parts and components it uses for American assembly from factories abroad.

The American automakers have also worked out cooperative agreements with overseas producers. The most ambitious of these is a joint venture of General Motors and Toyota, the New United Motor Manufacturing, Inc. (NUMMI). In 1985, the two auto giants opened the NUMMI plant in Fremont, California, and it now produces about 200,000 Chevrolet Novas a year.

The automakers, and the United Auto Workers Union, also responded to foreign competition with demands for trade protection. Ford, Chrysler, and the union were especially vehement about the need for trade barriers. In 1981, under the threat of Congressional legislation, the Japanese agreed to limit automobile exports to the United States to about 1.8 million cars and trucks a year. The "voluntary" restraint agreement has been extended repeatedly, and it has allowed American automakers to rebuild their profitability substantially. The export restraints, of course, increased the cost of cars in the United States by reducing the supply of cheaper Japanese imports; it is estimated that in 1984 the loss to consumers was $5.8 billion, while the gain to the American firms was $2.6 billion. Even so, the number of automobile workers in the United States has dropped by almost 200,000 since 1979, as automakers continue to cut costs.[5]

The American steel industry, even more than the automobile industry, has been completely remade by international economic integration. Developing countries, along with Japan, have built modern steel mills staffed by workers who earn far less than their American counterparts. American mills are still very efficient; in 1985, they used an average of 6.5 man-hours to produce a ton of steel—well below the Japanese and German figures and half the South Korean industry. Yet steel labor costs in the United States are still double what they are in Japan and Western Europe and as much as ten times what they are in East Asia and Latin America, where average steel wages are two or three dollars an hour.[6] Although steel industry wages have dropped by a fifth against inflation since 1982, labor still costs five times more per ton of steel in the United States than in South Korea. Labor costs are not the only problem; steel consumption has declined since the introduction of plastic, and the American steel industry has been notoriously slow to introduce new techniques and equipment. The central problem, however, is that few investors are willing to build or modernize an American steel mill when it has slim chances of being internationally competitive.

The steel industry's troubles have persisted despite a string of trade barriers dating back to the 1960s. The industry has used a wide variety of tactics to keep foreign steel out of the country, from court suits to the Carter administration's Trigger Price Mechanism. Since 1982, the Reagan administration has forced most of the world's steel-makers to agree to "voluntary" export restraints. The agreements now cover the European Community, Japan, and a number of developing and Socialist countries—all in all, four-fifths of all imported steel. Still, the American industry is barely profitable, and hardly competitive.

The inability of the United States to sustain its century-long leadership in integrated steel-making has forced a complete restructuring of the industry. Since 1973, American steel output has dropped by a third, and employment has gone from over 600,000 to barely 200,000; the United Steelworkers Union is half its former size. By 1990, American steel-making capacity will be half its 1973 levels. Virtually the only profitable segment of the industry is the recycling of scrap metal in "mini-mills," where wages are generally below half what they are in the big unionized mills.

The large steel companies have slashed wages, closed mills, and expanded foreign ties; many of them have also begun to get out of steel. National Steel sold its Weirton, West Virginia, mill to its employees; LTV's Jones and Laughlin Steel merged with Republic Steel and then LTV declared bankruptcy, as have McLouth Steel and Wheeling-Pittsburgh Steel. U.S. Steel so reduced its reliance on the industry—steel now accounts for less than a third of its operations—that it changed its name to USX. The steel-makers also scrambled for preferential deals with foreign producers. Japan's Nippon Kokan owns half of National Steel, Nisshin Steel owns two-thirds of Wheeling-Pittsburgh, and LTV has a joint venture with Sumitomo Metal. Inland Steel and Nippon Steel are building a $400 million rolling mill together. USX and South Korea's government-owned Pohang Iron and Steel Company have a $500 million joint venture to bring raw steel from Korea to be finished in California, a move that Lynn Williams, president of the United Steelworkers Union, called "another step in the disintegration of industrial America."[7]

Since 1970, demands by both capitalists and labor unions for trade protection have grown dramatically. The extraordinary strength of the dollar between 1981 and 1985 magnified both import competition and demands for relief, but the longer-term problems did not go away when the dollar declined.

Every major import-competing industry has requested trade restrictions, and some have obtained them. Producers have found creative ways to keep imports out, such as mutually negotiated quotas or "Buy American" legislation. Four domestic cement manufacturers ingeniously argued that the construction of a northern California port facility to import cement would have an adverse environmental impact, filed suit to halt port construction, and eventually stopped the project.[8] Similar concerns about international competition led manufacturers and farmers to attack the Federal Reserve, and the banking system more generally, for a monetary policy in the early 1980s that strengthened the dollar, cheapened imports, and raised the cost of capital.

Much of industrial America has indeed pressed for trade protection, and has received it. Gary Hufbauer and his associates at the Institute for International Economics have done a detailed study of "special protection"—trade barriers beyond normal tariffs and restrictions—given to thirty-one industries in the United States. Protected industries ranged from steel, auto, and textiles to peanuts and canned tuna. Hufbauer and his coauthors found that in 1984 special protection affected over one-fifth of American imports, $67 billion in all; restraints reduced imports by $44 billion and cost consumers $53 billion. In textiles and clothing, for example, negotiated trade restrictions reduced American imports by $27.9 billion—more than half; American production was one-third higher than it would have been, and the restraints brought producers $22 billion in additional earnings.[9]

On balance, however, the United States remains relatively open to international goods movements, and of course capital flows are unrestricted. Many corporations facing import competition are thus able to react by diversifying their investments. Robert Galvin, chief executive of Motorola, Inc., notes that international competition has led the $5 billion electronics firm to shift almost half its jobs abroad: "We will do what we have to in order to survive." Yet Galvin points out that the firm's survival has come at the country's expense: "That survival includes a process of defection. We are defecting from this country." Galvin charges bitterly that government unwillingness to face the problem will have dire effects: "By failing to stand up for American industry the American government is inadvertently letting American industry walk out of this society."[10]

International economic competition has posed serious challenges to firms all over the United States. Many have fought for government protection, and some have obtained it. Even those who were unable to secure government support might gradually, like Motorola, modernize or dismantle their American operations in favor of either labor-saving techniques or overseas production. And most of the industries that did receive trade protection took advantage of the respite from international competition to reduce labor costs, diversify, or invest abroad.

The implication is that firms will adjust by shifting production, albeit with difficulty, but the brunt of the transformation's burden will be borne by workers whose jobs will disappear. While many affected firms have been able to adjust to international competition, it is harder for workers to do so. Labor, after all, is not as mobile as capital, either geographically or between sectors. Workers often have skills specific to a particular industry, and even if they do not, the prospect of moving a family across the country in search of a job that may not exist is hardly attractive for unemployed workers with little or no savings.

Howard Samuel, president of the AFL-CIO's Industrial Union Department, is bitter about the effects of global economic integration on American labor. As he puts it, "You do not have to tell the average manufacturing worker what international competition has done to American industry. He has been on the front line of the changes, and he carries the heaviest burden. Unlike managers and professionals and entrepreneurs, the factory worker cannot meet the competition by shifting production overseas or by merging with another company or by closing plants and concentrating on more profitable lines. He has only his skills, his family, and his home, and that is where he has to make his stand. If his skills do not suffice, he has a brief interval of income support, without health or hospital benefits, a one in twenty chance for some retraining, and an 80 percent likelihood of finding either no job or one that pays substantially less than what he was previously earning."[11]

Whether it emanates from labor, management, or a coalition of both; whether it takes the form of protectionism, opposition to U.S. participation in the IMF, or animosity toward international banking, economic nationalism is once more an important force in the American political economy. The dramatic changes going on in the world and in the U.S. economy have called forth a reaction that may well threaten the stability of the global financial structure, as well as the interests of American international bankers.

The changes underway in the U.S. economy, and the roots of American opposition to international economic integration, are reflected in the desert town of Fontana, California. There, on arid wasteland fifty miles east of downtown Los Angeles, the Kaiser Steel Corporation built the biggest steel mill in the western United States during World War II. In 1979, Kaiser sank $250 million into a Basic Oxygen Furnace,

or BOF, to make raw steel; at its peak, the factory was turning out over 3 million tons of steel a year and had more than
8,000 workers. Today the BOF is closed, the mill no longer
makes steel, and Kaiser no longer owns the main facilities.
Foreign steel helped drive Kaiser's Fontana mill out of
business, but foreign capital and management, and foreign
steel, have revived it on a new basis. In August 1984, most
of the old factory was sold to an international consortium
called California Steel Industries, or CSI. California Steel is
owned by Japan's Kawasaki Steel and the Brazilian government's Companhia Vale do Rio Doce (CVRD). The two are
drawn together by a common interest in the Brazilian government-owned Tubarão steel mill north of Rio de Janeiro.
Kawasaki has a part interest in Tubarão, and CVRD is a
mining conglomerate that sells iron ore to Tubarão. The old
Kaiser factory now operates as a mill to finish raw steel that
CSI imports, primarily from the Tubarão mill. The steel-
making itself, which is highly labor intensive, takes place in
Tubarão, which has an annual capacity of 3 million tons. To
square the circle, most of the money used to build the
Tubarão mill was borrowed abroad, and CVRD is also a
major international debtor.

The decline and rise of Kaiser/California Steel began, indirectly, when international banks lent CVRD and Tubarão
the money to mine iron ore and produce steel. Brazil's low
wages and plentiful iron ore, and Kawasaki Steel's high technology, helped make the Tubarão plant very efficient, and
the growth of similar steel mills around the world led steel
consumers in the United States to abandon Kaiser. Today the
debt-financed steel mill in Brazil ships one-quarter of its
production to California Steel, which works the raw steel
into finished products for sale in the United States. The process has, albeit indirectly, shifted the labor-intensive portion
of the Fontana factory's operations to Brazil but kept the

final stages and marketing functions in the United States. Kaiser's mill had over 8,000 employees at its peak; today CSI has about 800. Meanwhile, the brand-new Tubarão factory in Brazil has 6,000 workers making roughly the same quantities of raw steel as the old Kaiser mill used to.

I visited California Steel on a sweltering April day in 1985, just a few months after the mill began operations. I spent most of the day with Paulo Burnier, the CSI president and representative of CVRD. Burnier is an expansive Brazilian in his late forties, a mining engineer who has been a CVRD employee since 1962, except for a period in the 1970s when he fell out of favor with the company's military president. Burnier has worked in iron and steel, bauxite and aluminum, and uranium.

Brazil's CVRD was interested in California Steel Industries for two important reasons, Burnier told me. First, the mining firm needs to sell ore, and the old Kaiser mill had been a major CVRD customer. "CVRD had a contract to provide Kaiser with iron ore," Burnier explained. "When Kaiser closed, this caused problems for us. Kawasaki was already interested because they are a partner in Tubarão and have a contractual obligation to export slabs from Tubarão." For CVRD the consortium offered the opportunity to replace one customer with another, for, as Burnier noted, "Tubarão is a major customer for our iron ore. Also the price was very good—$110 million; to construct all of this new would cost $600 to $700 million."

A second attraction for CVRD, Burnier said, was that the project could be coordinated with the needs of a CVRD-owned shipping line. The line, Docenave, transports Brazilian ore to overseas customers and brings other products back to Brazil. CSI's plans fit Docenave's routes, because Brazil imports coal from the United States and Canada. Docenave ships, Burnier said, "can come here, drop off slabs, and go back to Brazil with coal."

California Steel is a complex international partnership. CVRD sells iron ore to the government-owned Tubarão mill, in which Kawasaki has part interest. The raw steel is brought to California on CVRD ships, finished at CSI, and sold in the American market. And, of course, much of the financing for CVRD and Tubarão came from international financial markets: CVRD owes about $1.5 billion abroad, Tubarão another billion dollars or so.

CSI's finishing mill uses little American labor. The entire hot strip mill, which heats the steel slabs to 2400° F and rolls them down to thin coils, is manned by no more than a dozen workers, who supervise most of the process from an instrument panel at one end of the enormous building. A visitor to the plant sees only a few American workers and Japanese technicians.

Burnier summarizes the mill's operations: "CSI imports steel—two-thirds from Brazil. We locate the finishing operations here, use advanced technology from the Japanese, American labor in the finishing part of the process, American energy, American coal, and American sales management." Some of the details of the process are ironic. The old Kaiser mill's distance from port facilities was one of the reasons for its uncompetitiveness but, Burnier told me, the Kaiser mill was originally built far inland to protect it from Japanese bombardment during World War II; a leading Japanese firm is now part-owner of the factory.

Paulo Burnier concludes from his international industrial experience that national borders must erode.

> The Western world cannot survive economically with this nationalism garbage. Each country has its own vocation; we have to make associations between countries to get the cheapest costs possible in order for everybody to profit. Sometimes it's difficult. But people in the United States have to realize that the world is more and more international.
> I saw what's happening now in the States happen in Brazil a

long time ago, with foreign companies coming in and buying up parts of the economy. When I was a kid I used to use a soap called "Carnaval," very popular in Brazil. It was a big Brazilian soap company. When the old owner died, though, the first ones to knock on the door after the funeral were Unilever, which ended up buying the company. Of course, the United States is not Brazil. But the process is beginning.

The decline of Kaiser and other firms like it, and the rise of such new international consortia as CSI, is a striking result of the increasing integration of the United States into international markets for goods and capital. California Steel Industries is a microcosm of the rapidly changing world economy, in which the United States has become more and more a consumer of foreign-made industrial products and a financier of foreign industry. These changes are neither costless nor painless. Indeed, international economic integration has caused dislocations that strengthen sentiment hostile to both global markets and those who profit by them.

The death of Kaiser Steel's Fontana mill, and its rebirth as a Japanese-Brazilian joint venture to process Brazilian steel slabs, most directly affected the Kaiser workers who were laid off in 1983. To hear their side of the story, I spoke with a group of five former Kaiser workers, none of them currently employed in industry. We met in the hall of the Steelworkers' Oldtimers Foundation, a benevolent association set up by the Kaiser union local to carry out community work twenty years ago, when the steel mill dominated the economic and political life of the surrounding area. Kaiser is gone, the union local is deactivated, and only the Oldtimers Foundation with a network of self-help groups remains.

The former steelworkers recognize imported steel as an important proximate cause of the plant closure. Irv Russom, a former chairman of the local's hospital and pension committee, remembers, "There was no way we could sell steel for what they could import it and sell it for."

The men pointed out, however, that when the mill ran into problems, the union local tried hard to keep it open. Productivity committees were formed to involve workers in boosting production, but management, the former union officials said, lost interest in the committees. The local's attempt to forego cost-of-living raises was turned down by the international union, afraid it would set a bad precedent. In 1981, the local tried to buy the plant through an Employee Stock Ownership Program, or ESOP, although the international union was again unenthusiastic. The local succeeded in raising half the money it needed, borrowing much of it from a British insurance company and a Canadian bank. When the Mexican debt crisis hit in the summer of 1982, however, the Canadian bank decided against further international exposure and backed out. The mill closed a year later.

The former Kaiser workers all believed that unprincipled management helped kill the mill. Many of the firm's executives, they say, had little incentive to keep the plant open. As Irv Russom said, "Some of the corporate heads of Kaiser got out of there with half-million-dollar payoffs. They're set; they've got their golden parachutes, but the workers are just out in the cold." Gary Lord, former local publicity chairman, noted bitterly, "And they're the ones who had control over whether the company was going down or not. They had a way out; they made more money by shutting it down than they would have if it ran."

The men are angry at management for the plant's failure and for a squeeze on them that continued even after they were laid off. In the complex financial dealings by which the company changed hands, the former employees were forced to accept cuts in their original benefit programs. "They had a gun to our heads," Irv Russom said. "First they threatened to take away the health plan altogether. Then they said that if the merger didn't fly, it could jeopardize our pensions.

They've reduced every retiree's health plan 30 or 40 percent; we're in litigation now over our health plan. Instead of
trying to help people who are out of work, they're trying to
cut back on benefits. Most of us are waiting for the other shoe
to drop; we're afraid they're going to start screwing with our
pensions." Indeed, early in 1987 Kaiser missed a payment to
its insurance company, and 5,000 former employees lost
their medical benefits.

Dino Papavero, president of the Kaiser local from 1970 to
1976 and now head of the Oldtimers Foundation, is indig-
nant. "On top of it all, three months ago Kaiser declared a
profit of about $47 million. But they haven't made one ounce
of steel." Gary Lord shakes his head, "I took big cuts; they're
making money; and all the time they're telling me they're
going broke."

Dino Papavero was outraged at the speculative profits
made amidst the workers' suffering. "This headline right
here tears me up," he said, picking up a copy of the local
newspaper with a front-page story entitled "Frates' Kaiser
profit: 4,000%." Indeed, in 1984, after the Fontana mill's
closure, Kaiser Steel was taken over in a leveraged buyout
by Tulsa investor Joseph Frates, who hived off various parts
of the Fontana property, including California Steel. Frates'
group put up a million dollars of its own money—the rest was
borrowed—and realized a $41 million profit, according to
the article. "There's something wrong with that," Papavero
said, pointing at the headline. "A 4,000 percent profit, and
this guy never worked a graveyard shift in his life. A lot of
people depended upon this industry for their livelihood, and
management removed the mainstay of a community of
50,000. There seems to be no concern for the employees
who gave twenty-five or thirty years of service to that corporation.

"There's something wrong with the system," Dino

Papavero concluded. "But how are you going to change Frates, who got 4,000 percent on his money? He thinks the system is great. We think it's a mess, but Frates has more weight than we have." To Gary Lord the injustice is clear: "Frates doesn't supply any more to the national economy than any one of us—probably less. He only eats so many beans and so much bread. He doesn't own a car—he's leasing it and getting tax credits on it. He doesn't contribute as much to the national economy as we do."

Kaiser's former employees are pessimistic about the economic outlook and about the future of working people. Jim Elliott, a former vice-president of the local union, Gary Lord, and Irv Russom had just finished being retrained as paralegals, but were cynical about job possibilities for fifty-year-old paralegals in the California desert. "I read in *Life* magazine," said Elliott sardonically, "that in fifteen years the second-best job you could have in the United States, after computer programmer, will be as a paralegal. So we've all decided that if we can hold out for another fifteen years we should be able to get good jobs." Gary Lord ticked off the years on his fingers: "Heck, I'll be ready to retire by then."

Dino Papavero extrapolated from the local experience to national trends: "This country is coming to a lower standard of living. If heavy industry deteriorates, the living standard of the vast majority of the population will reflect that downward trend. Do we want a living standard in this society below Russia's, or even China's? If we don't, we're going to have to do something to regenerate heavy industry. But right now there's something wrong with the system; industry is receiving a lot more money for raiding the U.S. Treasury than for making a product."

Papavero has thought of the political alternatives. "Somewhere down the road we have to get the government to maintain the industrial might and productivity of this country. That's hard for us to do, because we don't have the economic resources these large companies do. But unless we change something in this society, there's going to be no alternative. We're going to see mergers and greater influence by the multinational corporations, along with a decline of our standard of living. I don't know what the alternative is, but it has to be political—it might have to be some kind of revolution."

These half dozen men are quintessential middle Americans. All are white, between forty and fifty-five years old, family men with community roots; Gary Lord says proudly that his family has lived within twenty-five miles of Fontana since 1849. They and their fellow Kaiser employees had steady, good-paying jobs; it was not unusual, they say, for a Kaiser worker to earn $35,000 a year with overtime and incentive pay. Some put in thirty years at Kaiser; none has more to show for it than endangered health and pension benefits, and a residue of bitterness toward the captains of industry and finance. As we said good-bye, Jim Elliott summed up the experience of the three that had undergone retraining to prepare them for the economy's structural transformation: "We just got out of school May 1. We used to be unemployed steelworkers; now we're unemployed paralegals." Gary Lord added, "But in fifteen years we'll have good jobs. If we're still alive."

The ordeal of Kaiser's former employees illustrates some of the effects of global economic integration, and their anger exemplifies some of the dangers faced by American international business people. One potential threat, from both labor and capital in industries that face competition from imports, is the rise of economic nationalism. Yet many workers—like Kaiser's unemployed—are far less bitter about foreigners than they are about American businesses that appear to be abandoning their employees. This is the vertical pressure that international investors face, as goods and capital mobility threaten the livelihood of many American workers.

The shifting position of the United States in the world economy is indeed changing the American economy itself. As new industrial centers have eroded the American edge in much of manufacturing, firms have moved away from traditional industry and toward the production of goods higher in technology or toward the provision of services. The center of gravity of the American economy has shifted from industry to such classically white-collar activities as research and development, telecommunications, management services, finance, real estate, and the professions. Even as American steel-makers lay off their production workers, American banks and corporations with expanding overseas interests hire many more bookkeepers, clerks, lawyers, and traders. Between 1979 and 1985, in fact, while manufacturers in the United States reduced their payrolls by 1.5 million workers, service-producing industries expanded theirs by almost 10 million.

Changes in the structure of the U.S. economy will have a profound effect on the domestic social order. The structural transformation of the U.S. economy may seriously affect American living standards, equality, labor organization, and the political system itself.

There is no question that the standard of living of the average American has suffered over the past fifteen years. Correcting for inflation, average weekly earnings of private nonagricultural workers rose by nearly two-thirds between World War II and 1973, but have since dropped by almost 15 percent; median family income expressed in today's dollars peaked at over $28,000 a year in 1973, and is now 6 percent below that. Generally slow economic growth may be at the root of the deterioration, but the decline of manufacturing has probably contributed to the downward trend, because the gap between manufacturing and service wages is large and is increasing. After World War II, weekly retail-trade earnings were over two-thirds weekly manufacturing earnings, but now they are less than half—even though manufacturing wages are themselves depressed.

Whether or not living standards continue to decline, there is little question that the structural transformation of the U.S. economy is making income less equally distributed. One of the most distinctive social and political features of the United States has long been the relatively high pay of un-skilled and semiskilled industrial workers. The ability of steelworkers and autoworkers to afford a middle-class life-style leveled the American social structure and held out hope of social mobility to the working class. The decline of manufacturing employment has nearly closed off this ave-nue to advancement, while the rise of headquarters jobs in major international banks and corporations has opened up new opportunities for the very highly educated. Income has become substantially more concentrated since 1970, as the proportion of low-paying jobs in the economy has increased while good-paying production jobs have almost disappeared. In the late 1960s, the richest one-fifth of Americans earned seven times more on average than the poorest one-fifth; today the difference is more than nine to one.[12]

Growing income disparities have important political im-plications. The social mobility of manufacturing workers, indeed, served to dampen the working-class unrest that most advanced industrial societies experience; the United States is, after all, the only developed nation where workers do not typically support a Socialist or Communist party. For many years, firms subject to little domestic or international compe-tition found it relatively easy to strike bargains with their labor force, and the insularity of the U.S. economy, coupled with the domination of many industries by a few companies, allowed for a great deal of sectoral cooperation between labor and management.

Increasing economic openness subjected even the most oligopolistic of goods producers to competition, and the comfortable deals struck with labor began to come unstuck under the weight of international constraints. Associate Deputy Under Secretary of Labor John Stepp, pointing out that "foreign competition has changed the name of the game," argues that American labor relations "are in a period of great turbulence, perhaps the most turbulent time since the 1930s. We are witnessing the transition from a post-New Deal labor-relations system into something quite different." The National Association of Manufacturers' Randolph Hale agrees on the reasons for new labor-management relations that he calls "survival" or "reality" bargaining: "Markets have changed. Global competition is the new reality. With some exceptions, Americans are not competing successfully in today's world economy."[13]

The American labor movement is on the defensive. Less than one in five workers is now in a union, the lowest proportion of the labor force since the New Deal. Most industrial contracts in the 1980s have forced workers to accept wage reductions, changes in work rules, two-tier wage systems in which new employees are hired at far lower wages than veterans, and a wide variety of other concessions. The AFL-CIO's Howard Samuel also indicates the global origins of the problem: "The most pressing new reality in industrial relations has been the internationalization of the American economy." He is bitter about management's response; the past few years have been, he says, "a time of sham and hypocrisy when nonunion employers croon about collaboration, when giant corporations with union relationships illegally fire union supporters in their nonunion plants, when big business demands worker concessions to meet international competition and then gives second helpings to their top executives."[14]

Labor is bound to search for new strategies to confront the changed environment, and these new strategies may have broad political effects. Indeed, some studies show that labor movements in industrial countries open to world trade are more class based than those in relatively closed economies, which tend to organize on sectoral, regional, or ethnic lines. This is because in an open economy sectoral bargains—very high wages in the auto sector, for example—will rapidly be washed out by international competition. The implication is that increased economic openness in the United States may drive workers together politically, and set them more decisively against the business community.[15] Racial minorities, too, are likely to be relatively disfavored by structural adjustment, since they have been overrepresented among unskilled and semiskilled factory workers and underrepresented in higher-wage white-collar occupations; one in eight steelworkers and autoworkers has generally been black, but only one in twenty-five computer workers.[16]

This growing economic polarization of the United States may feed conflict among classes, regions, and racial groups. A. Gary Shilling, a New York economic consultant, told the *New York Times,* "People don't want to throw in the towel on the American dream. Most Americans seem to regard as their birthright their belief that they will live higher on the hog than their parents. They don't want to admit that what they thought was happening economically no longer is. When they are finally forced to bite the bullet, there could be a tough situation with potential social and political overtones. When people realize that their living standards are declining on a long-term basis, they'll be very upset. When they see that one group is continuing to gain in purchasing power—that is, management and entrepreneurs—they're going to feel that this adds insult to injury. If the trend toward inequality gets bad enough," Shilling concluded, the result might be "a renewal of the class resentment we had in the 1930s during the Depression. Then there might be a big movement to spread the wealth."[17]

Political strife in the United States worries many American international bankers, for they recognize that the domestic reaction to economic distress might involve attacks on international finance and the openness of the international economy. C. Fred Bergsten—a prominent member of the foreign economic policy establishment, head of the Institute for International Economics, and veteran of the National Security Council and the Treasury Department in the Nixon and Carter administrations—regards domestic political trends as crucial to the continuation of current economic openness. As Bergsten put it in 1980, "The need to sustain domestic support for a continued strong U.S. involvement in the world economy is the most critical item of all on the agenda for the future . . . This will be a continuing battle for U.S. policy officials but an essential ingredient for an effective international economic policy for the 1980s."[18] The economic and human forces created in Fontana, and hundreds of similar communities around the country, will be central to this continuing battle.

Through the furor over America's international economic role, and over its domestic economic order, American international bankers continue to maintain their belief in the desirability of free markets at home and abroad. In fact, there are large constituencies in favor of continued international economic integration, and in support of current economic trends in the United States. Support for market-oriented policies at home and abroad comes, obviously, from those able to succeed in international competition. While many firms and workers are hard pressed by international markets, others have done well in them. Firms with global economic commitments, and employees whose livelihood depends on these international commitments, oppose attempts to block the operation of international economic forces.

The future preferred by competitive, internationally integrated industries, led by American international bankers, is the continuation of the structural change now going on, a gradual "deindustrialization" of the United States as the economy shifts into international and domestic services. This path assumes a redoubled American commitment to abide by the decisions of international markets and keep wages, prices, and profits globally competitive. If the United States and its partners agree to allow markets to take their course, the argument goes, the result will be higher income for all.

Even the strongest supporters of allowing international trends to shape the U.S. economy recognize that the process is not painless. Charles Meissner is sympathetic to the plight of the unemployed: "If you take the train to Washington you see the empty factories; Philadelphia is like going through an empty wasteland. We are seeing a huge shift in labor from the Rust Belt to the Sun Belt. There's been agony; society has passed on the structural adjustment cost to the individuals who can probably bear the cost least—they have had to move, they have had to resettle, they have had to retrain. But it has taken place."

Despite its social and personal costs, Meissner argues, the current changes in the American economy are inevitable. Meissner, like the rest of the American financial community, believes that the United States must get out of labor-intensive industry and into high technology and services. "Because we're the country that introduces most of the new technology," Meissner says, "the way we create jobs is to continue to introduce new technology. What is high-tech now is going to be medium technology fifty or sixty years from now, and someone else is going to produce it. Fifty years from now Mexico and Brazil will be producing the computers and the airplanes. Therefore we need huge research and development costs. We should be exploring space in fifty years, mining the moon, setting up interplanetary something-or-others, taking our frontiers someplace else."

International financial leaders consistently argue against any erosion of international economic integration. One of the foremost campaigners against trade protection, for example, has been the Federal Reserve's former chairman Paul Volcker, who has repeatedly recognized the problem but argued for international solutions: "Sectors of the American economy exposed to international competition—that is, much of industry, mining, and agriculture—are paying a heavy price. . . . Out of sheer frustration, as things now stand, pressures are building in the United States for protectionist measures, even among industries and segments of the labor movement that traditionally have supported liberal trading policies. Such a response would deal with symptoms, not causes. In the end, like inflationary policies, protectionism would only complicate the problem."[19]

The most serious challenge to America's international financial institutions is the growth of "economic nationalism," including everything from trade protectionism to distaste for the IMF. The economic and political interests of American international business people and internationalist policymakers force them into conflict with those who insist that government defend uncompetitive industries from international economic rivals. Opposition to economic internationalism is indeed strong. Major portions of the business community and of the labor movement are disenchanted with exposure to the international economy, and popular support for international economic integration, never very deep in the insular American political system, has eroded continually for over a decade. A mid-1985 *New York Times*–CBS News poll, for example, indicated that half the American public felt that trade hurts their communities, while over two-thirds believed that foreign trade costs jobs for the United States, and considered limiting imports a good idea.[20]

Charles Meissner worries that the American political system may simply be incapable of forging a domestic consensus on an internationalist foreign economic policy.

> It's what I call institutional sclerosis: The political structure is such that until a crisis, when the whole thing blows up, you don't get institutional changes. The political structure is too responsive to local needs and not responsive to macro needs.
>
> The Congress and the executive branch have continued to ignore the problem. The lack of commitment to the global system has been worse in this administration. And yet the real issue for the United States is, if we want the benefits of the international system that accrue to our business and security, we have to take greater responsibility in our domestic policies, to take into consideration the international ramifications of domestic decisions. We don't do that, and we're continuing not to do it.

Political strife over domestic and international economic issues is bound to escalate. The future is likely to be conflictual, as economic nationalists battle economic internationalists and the economically advantaged confront the economically disadvantaged.

In theory, of course, there is nothing to stop a society from evolving from a closed economy based on manufacturing to an open economy based on overseas earnings, trade, and services. In practice, however, this transition requires such massive shifts of capital, labor, and skills that it inevitably generates resistance.

The British experience with industrial decline is instructive. As the United Kingdom lost its international industrial primacy in the late 1800s, it rapidly expanded its international investments; in the years before World War I, about half of the country's capital went overseas. The country led the world in international finance and other services. London was—as it is today—the world's financial center, headquarters to a global trading and investment empire. Great Britain looked increasingly like a rentier state, living off its sophisticated financial, informational, and trading skills, and off its massive overseas investments.

The "deindustrialization" of the United Kingdom, however, led to domestic conflict. As the south prospered, the industrial north struggled against foreign competition; neither industrial capitalists nor industrial workers were willing or able to abandon their homes and lines of business in favor of postindustrial London and the Home Counties around it.

After World War I, bitter disputes raged along two axes: internationalists against nationalists, and class against class. Financial and commercial parties that wanted to maintain their overseas interests even at the expense of national industry fought for free trade, the gold standard, and international economic cooperation. Domestic industrialists and many workers demanded trade protection and government support, often by closing the British Empire to foreign competitors. The labor movement, under continued pressure on wages, took increasingly confrontational positions against management, and insisted that the government intervene to maintain working-class living standards.

Acrimonious economic debates between internationalist

finance and protectionist industry, and between the privileged and the disadvantaged, have torn the United Kingdom apart since the 1920s. Conflict has, if anything, increased in recent years, as positions have hardened. Since 1978, Britain has lost a third of its manufacturing jobs. Unemployment nationally is at 11 percent, and in parts of the north it is twice that. Another one-third of the labor force is employed but has no job security. The most obvious result has been a rise in class-based, regional, and racial strife—even violence.[21] The country's chronic political and economic problems have helped make Britain the slowest-growing industrial economy in the world for seventy years. The world's former industrial leader now has the lowest income per person of any advanced capitalist country.

The United Kingdom is not the United States, and in any event one precedent is hardly sufficient on which to base predictions, but Britain's misfortune is surely a warning about the seriousness of current events. In the United States, the confluence of structural change and cyclical economic downturns could drive the country into hostile camps and unprecedented sociopolitical struggle. Facile assertions of the desirability of structural adjustment notwithstanding, the political and economic future of the United States is hardly settled.

The postwar American political economy has begun to circle back on itself. After World War II, the United States constructed an international economic order based on the free movement of goods and capital across national borders. The highly competitive American economy benefited enormously from the system. Global economic integration, however, stimulated American goods imports, overseas investment, and foreign lending. New centers of industry abroad grew, and much of the U.S. economy could not compete with them. The effects of international finance, investment, and trade on American employment and living standards have eroded much of the pre-existing support for international economic integration. A consensus forged with great difficulty in the Depression and World War II, that the United States should support economic internationalism, was so successful at moving capital and industrial production out of the United States that the consensus has begun to break down.

For forty years America's international bankers have been at the center of a world economy whose organizing principle was the free movement of capital and goods, and whose slogan was interdependence. Since 1970, the accelerating pace of economic change that the postwar economic order fostered has given rise to conflicts both between and within nations over everything from trade protection to foreign debt and currency values. In both international and domestic arenas, the near future will be a time of crucial debates and battles over the shape of domestic and international politics and economics.

The leaders of international finance, along with their allies in the business community, in government, and elsewhere, hope and work for a deepening of contemporary international economic integration. Yet the market globalism of the world's bankers confronts other interests at stake. On one axis, opponents challenge the bankers' globalism, and call for national or regional protection against foreign competition. On another axis, opponents contest the affluence of the bankers and their allies, and demand social and political intervention to redistribute the wealth that market forces

have concentrated. The first axis divides economic internationalists from economic nationalists; the second axis sets
wealth against poverty. The conflict between opposing
poles, on both dimensions, will determine the future of the
American, and of the international, political economy.

8

Conclusion

One hundred years ago American bankers had little international significance. The world's leading financial markets in London, Paris, and Berlin regarded American banks only as conduits for their lucrative American investments. In the last years of the nineteenth century and the early years of the twentieth, New York bankers, led by J. P. Morgan, gradually built up foreign operations. Still, most of this embryonic American international finance was concentrated in the Caribbean area, and it was very much secondary to the bankers' principal interests in industrial finance inside the United States.

During and after World War I, American bankers shot to the pinnacle of the world economy. With the House of Morgan in the lead, American international financiers helped restructure European economies, papered over the war debts controversy, and lent billions of dollars to bankroll rapid economic growth in Europe and Latin America. Yet the bankers' worldwide economic interests often conflicted with the concerns and ideas of American isolationists, who blocked many of the policies preferred by the economic internationalists. Political divisions over America's international economic role reached their high point in the early years of the Depression, when Congress voted sky-high tariffs that helped bring the fragile international financial system crashing down.

From the depths of the Depression, American financial leaders and foreign policymakers cautiously began rebuilding the international financial order. American political support for economic internationalism grew in the late 1930s, and especially during and after World War II. The war destroyed most of the country's fiercest economic competitors and made trade liberalization less threatening. With the onset of the Cold War, international economic cooperation was presented to the public as a necessary weapon in the anti-Soviet arsenal.

Since World War II, American international bankers and their counterparts in Western Europe and Japan have constructed the largest international financial system in world history. Most contemporary international banking has migrated "offshore," to Euromarkets that are largely independent of any single national government. Technological advances allow international fund transfers, lending, and currency trading to take place almost instantaneously between markets thousands of miles apart.

Modern global banking, and the new international economic realities it has created, challenges the world's political systems. The linkage of national money and capital markets constrains government policies in all countries; billions of dollars ricochet from country to country in response to changes in international interest rates and currency values. Massive international loans helped finance rapid industrial development in parts of the Third World, and made many of the developed world's traditional industrial plants uncompetitive. Since 1980, the U.S. government has become the world's largest international debtor, and the United States as a whole has become a net debtor nation for the first time since World War I.

In virtually every nation, the consequence of international financial integration has been domestic political conflict among groups with contending economic interests. It has created or reinforced sectors, firms, investors, and workers whose livelihood depends on the free movement of capital and goods across borders. But global financial integration has endangered the interests of other groups whose well-being is threatened by exposure to international competition for capital or markets. Within every national political system, demands for insulation from international markets clash with demands for access to them. As financial integration has speeded the structural transformation of the advanced industrial countries, the traditional industrial working class has come under mounting pressure. Political strife pits sector against sector and class against class.

Global banking has, in addition, fundamentally transformed the environment within which national and international politics are played out. Investors can react to political trends by shifting capital into or out of most national markets at will and in a matter of minutes. Government, corporate, and labor policies are thus constrained by the real or potential response of international financial markets.

Over the past hundred years, American international banking has emerged from obscurity before World War I to world leadership in the 1920s; then from failure in the 1930s to resurgence in the 1940s and 1950s; and finally, since 1960, to extraordinary international achievements. Each step in the process has led to important economic and political debates over such issues as gunboat diplomacy, isolationism, the Good Neighbor Policy, internationalism, and the Cold War. Contemporary international finance raises similarly important issues for the United States. International economic trends call into question the character of the American economy, its place in the world economy, and ultimately its domestic political and social order.

This book has attempted to clarify the complex issues contemporary international banking raises for global and national societies, and for the people in them. It has explored and explained the sources of today's international financial system, and examined the impact of modern international banking on domestic and international economics and politics.

Informed debate on the issues raised by contemporary international finance requires analytical care and factual accuracy. In the complex evolution of American international finance, it is not easy to separate the domestic from the international, the economic from the political, cause from effect. In fact, the two most common approaches to the problem are wrongheaded. One places undue emphasis on the role of individual bankers and politicians; the other exaggerates the immutability of economic forces.

Muckraking journalists and populists attribute the world's financial ills to a shadowy conspiracy of evil plutocrats. In this mysterious netherworld of power and influence, billionaire bankers gather to determine the fate of the world, plotting to subvert national interests and human progress. Right-wing demagogues accuse international bankers of aiding and abetting the un-American aims of One Worlders and Trilateralists. Left-wing moralists impute to international financiers a perverse taste for poverty and repression. So, contemporary international banking is often presented as a purely political, largely conspiratorial phenomenon.

This, of course, ignores the role of real economic forces

that act independently of individual design. Most of the evils that financial yellow journalists ascribe to corporate conspirators—limits on the freedom of action of national governments, foreign purchases of American assets, austerity programs in the Third World, plant closings in the United States—are the simple result of markets at work. No nefarious plot is needed to drive American steel corporations to insist that American steelworkers accept lower wages; international competition forces the firms to either reduce labor costs or go bankrupt. Most trends in the U.S. economy are determined by economic realities, not by a devious cabal.

Conspiracy theories can neither explain nor solve the problems of the American political economy, for they ignore the central importance of objective economic factors. In a market economy, firms—including banks—are limited by the dictates of the marketplace and by the requirements of adequate profitability. American international bankers support global economic integration and international economic cooperation because their business depends on these things, not because they have abandoned American values. They and their counterparts elsewhere insist on Third World stabilization and austerity programs because their profitability is closely related to the economic performance of the major debtors, not because of some vendetta against the Latin American peasantry. American international bankers, like all business people, must work within markets which they can rarely affect.

This does not imply that market forces are somehow natural and immutable. The most common counterargument to conspiracy theories about international finance is an equally indefensible paean to the impersonal and inevitable magic of the marketplace. Financial apologists often present undiscriminating and self-serving assertions that markets are independent of other social forces, and that attempts to control market forces are bound to fail. This rank economism ignores the central importance of politics in establishing the environment within which markets operate, and often in determining market outcomes.

Markets, financial and otherwise, are subject to manipulation. Indeed, it would be inconsistent to assert that firms act simply to maximize profits and simultaneously to assume that their actions will be confined to the economic sphere. If profits can be increased by bribing politicians, publishing political propaganda, and colluding with other companies, profit-maximizing firms will mix market and nonmarket actions.

As long as there are markets, they will be susceptible to manipulation by powerful economic interests, and there is never equal access to the tools necessary for such manipulation. Postwar international financial integration did not simply happen of its own accord; international bankers with much to gain from it spent years in the political arena fighting for policies to suit their interests. The same could be said about Third World debt, the structural transformation of the U.S. economy, or international trade patterns; these are not examples of pure market forces at work, but rather a complex mix of social, political, and economic influences in which markets are both a tool and an independent factor.

Global financial integration poses real choices for society. The choices are not elucidated, however, by personalized tales of demon bankers, or by mindless oversimplifications about the beneficent inevitability of market forces. Individual bankers do operate within the relatively restrictive confines of markets they do not control. Yet bankers, like other people, act in the political and social spheres to strengthen their economic position. Economic affairs are not determined by conspiracy, but neither are they some sort of natural phenomenon, like gravity, that is immune to conscious social control.

Inaccurate diagnoses lead to ineffective prescriptions, in political economy as in medicine. The remedies proposed by conspiracy theorists and free marketeers are every bit as misguided as their explanations for the very real ills society faces.

Those who trace contemporary economic problems to the evils of omnipotent individuals have clear solutions: replace or reform the individuals in question, or reduce their omnipotence. Xenophobic or moralistic populists would force international banks and corporations to act with patriotism or with a social conscience. They might break large firms into smaller ones, subject bank directors to minute personal scrutiny, or sell corporate shares to employees.

Individual desires, however, have little to do with the operation of international financial markets. Global banks respond to economic forces that are largely independent of the bankers themselves, and their response is largely determined by the structure of the market they are in. Attempts to tinker with the identity, patriotism, or morality of individual bankers or financial policymakers will have little effect on the nature of international financial markets.

Personalistic denunciation and expiation cannot change international economic trends, but it is not necessary to accept all of these trends as unchangeable. Free-market fatalists insist that the market's decisions are inevitable and final. Most are glad of this; a few are simply resigned to it. Either way, the only alternative is to allow laws of supply and demand to operate, and to make the best of the inexorable result.

Nonetheless, economic forces are ultimately, eminently, subject to social and political control. After all, markets are social institutions, not physical phenomena, and they can be altered by human action. For those concerned about broad social issues, unencumbered markets are no more an immutable given than malaria or illiteracy.

In the final analysis, the underlying question raised by the recent trajectory and current activity of international finance is the extent to which markets are adequate institutions for the further development of modern societies. This is not the same as asking whether bankers are greedy or politicians are corrupt; it is a broader question about the things markets do well, and the things they may not be able to provide.

Markets are extraordinarily effective at forcing efficiency at the microeconomic level. They help squeeze as much as possible out of productive resources; investors, managers, and workers cannot ignore the market's demands that they perform to their potential. Market forces have thus been central to human progress, especially in leading to a more effective use of land, labor, and capital. The spread of markets and associated institutions dissolved the torpor of medieval Europe and drew the world's peoples together for the first time. Modern international financial markets have brought previously underutilized resources in dozens of nations into modern production, and have helped spread ideas, technology, and skills to people who desperately need them.

Nevertheless, the macroeconomic inefficiencies of markets can be staggering. The operation of markets can wreak havoc with the lives of millions as supply and demand search out their equilibrium. As market forces tear at existing social relations, they can cause massive dislocations—driving millions of peasants from the land, throwing millions of laborers out of work, idling countless factories. The cost of adapting to the marketplace can be very high for individuals, and for society as a whole. It is indeed hard to imagine that any marginal increase in microeconomic efficiency is worth the enormous waste represented today by 30 million unemployed in the industrial countries, and tens of millions more in the Third World—not to speak of the mills and farms abandoned to the vortex of international competitive pressures.

Modern society can ill afford, nor need it resign itself to, the losses inflicted on it by unbridled market forces. The global banking system is a marvel of complex coordination; there is no reason that the energies it expends in searching out marginal arbitrage opportunities could not be turned toward more directly socially useful activities. Financial markets on their own will not evolve in this direction; they reward the pursuit of narrower goals. It is up to broader social forces and actors to put to less narrow use the enormous energy and technological sophistication of modern international finance.

The politics of American international finance since 1890 demonstrates two important precepts of political economy, both relevant for the future: societies cannot do what is economically impossible, and just because something is economically possible does not mean it will be done. New economic possibilities are realized only when the social forces that support them are cohesive and powerful enough to defeat whatever opposition the new possibilities may provoke. Contemporary international banking has developed remarkable economic and informational tools. For American and international society to make full use of the extraordinary social potential of modern international finance will require the efforts of social and political forces capable of harnessing this potential for more general social purposes. This book is not designed to predict or propose specific means to this end, only to provide information and analysis that might help others to form appropriate opinions and lines of action.

The history of American international banking is not one of villains or saviors. The many remarkable individuals who contributed to the development of contemporary global financial markets all acted within the confines of economic and political institutions they did not create, and over which they had little control. International finance has largely developed as the result of impersonal economic forces. Yet at crucial junctures, conscious measures have altered the course of modern financial history—whether at Bretton Woods, Geneva, Washington, or Mexico City. The reality of contemporary American international finance does not rule out conscious social action, but rather demands a concerted effort to harness existing economic forces in ways that can improve the human condition.

Source Notes

1: The United States in the World Economy

1. Adam Smith, *The Wealth of Nations* (New York: Modern Library, 1937), 573, 576.

2: The Early Years of American International Banking

1. Richard O. Boyer and Herbert M. Morais, *Labor's Untold Story*, (New York: Cameron, 1955), 136–137.
2. Cited in Dana G. Munro, *Intervention and Dollar Diplomacy in the Caribbean 1900–1921* (Princeton: Princeton University Press, 1964), 77.
3. Ibid, 113.
4. Harry Scheiber, "World War I as Entrepreneurial Experience," *Political Science Quarterly* 84, no. 3 (September 1969): 488.
5. Herbert Croly, *Willard Straight* (New York: Macmillan, 1925), especially 197–408.
6. Cited in Lewis Corey, *The House of Morgan* (New York: G. Howard Watt, 1930), 228; see also Calvin Tomkins, *Merchants and Masterpieces* (New York: Dutton, 1970).
7. Cleona Lewis, *America's Stake in International Investments* (Washington: Brookings Institution, 1938), 341.
8. Alexander Hemphill, "America's Financial Position as Affected by the War," *Annals of the American Academy of Political and Social Science* 60 (July 1915): 119, 121.
9. John Milton Cooper, "The Command of Gold Reversed," *Pacific Historical Review* 45, no. 2 (May 1976): 215.
10. Thomas W. Lamont, "The Effect of the War on America's Financial Position," *Annals of the American Academy of Political and Social Science* 60 (July 1915): 118.
11. Cooper, *Command of Gold Reversed*, 219–221.

12. Roberta A. Dayer, "Strange Bedfellows: J. P. Morgan and Co., Whitehall and the Wilson Administration During World War I," *Business History* 18, no. 2 (July 1976): 135.

13. Scott Nearing and Joseph Freeman, *Dollar Diplomacy* (New York: B.W. Huebsch, 1925), 273.

14. A. J. Rosenthal, "Foreign Corporate Bonds in the American Market," *Annals of the American Academy of Political and Social Science* 88 (March 1920): 138; Otto Kahn, *Of Many Things* (New York: Boni and Liveright, 1926), 211.

15. James Sheldon, "The Need for American Investment in Foreign Securities," *Annals of the American Academy of Political and Social Science* 88 (March 1920): 115–117.

16. Thomas Lamont, *Across World Frontiers* (New York: Harcourt, Brace, 1951), 267; two outstanding historical accounts of the period are William C. McNeil, *American Money and the Weimar Republic* (New York: Columbia University Press, 1986), and Stephen Schuker, *The End of French Predominance in Europe* (Chapel Hill: University of North Carolina Press, 1976).

17. John Douglas Forbes, *J. P. Morgan, Jr.* (Charlottesville: University Press of Virginia, 1981), 145.

18. Shepard Morgan, "Conditions Precedent to the Settlement," *Proceedings of the Academy of Political Science* 14, no. 2 (January 1931): 7.

19. Thomas W. Lamont, "The Dawes Plan and European Peace," *Proceedings of the Academy of Political Science* 11, no. 2 (January 1925): 184, 182.

20. U.S. Congress, House of Representatives, Committee on Banking and Currency, Subcommittee on Domestic Finance, *Federal Reserve Structure and the Development of Monetary Policy, 1915–1935: Staff Report* (Washington: U.S. Government Printing Office, 1971), 60–61.

21. Lamont, *Across World Frontiers*, 221.

22. Thomas Ferguson, "From Normalcy to New Deal," *International Organization* 38, no. 1 (Winter 1984): 66.

23. Lamont, *Across World Frontiers*, 215.

24. Mary Jane Maltz, *The Many Lives of Otto Kahn* (New York: Macmillan, 1963), 204–205.

25. Norman H. Davis, "Trade Barriers and Customs Duties," *Proceedings of the Academy of Political Science* 12, no. 4 (January 1928): 71–73.

26. Joan Hoff Wilson, *American Business and Foreign Policy, 1920–1933* (Lexington: University Press of Kentucky, 1971), 70–75.

27. Forbes, *J. P. Morgan, Jr.*, 125.

28. Melvin Leffler, "The Origins of Republican War Debt Policy," *Journal of American History* 59, no. 3 (December 1972): 590.

29. Roberta Allbert Dayer, "The British War Debts to the United States and the Anglo-Japanese Alliance, 1920–1923," *Pacific Historical Review*

45, no. 4 (November 1976): 590; for Morgan on Harding, see Forbes, *J. P. Morgan, Jr.*, 115.

30. Jacob Viner, "Political Aspects of International Finance, *Journal of Business of the University of Chicago* 1, no. 2 (April 1928): 146.

31. Michael Straight, *After Long Silence* (New York: Norton, 1983), 24.

32. Forbes, *J. P. Morgan, Jr.*, 144, 126; Harold Nicolson, *Diaries and Letters 1930–1939* (London: Collins, 1966), 203.

33. Shepard Morgan, "Constructive Functions of the International Bank," *Foreign Affairs* 9 (July 1931): 583, 588.

34. *Survey of American Foreign Relations 1928* (New Haven: Yale University Press for the Council on Foreign Relations, 1928), 178.

35. Robert F. Smith, *The United States and Revolutionary Nationalism in Mexico 1916–1932* (Chicago: University of Chicago Press, 1972), 246.

36. Harold Nicolson, *Dwight Morrow* (New York: Macmillan, 1935), 142.

37. Nicolson, *Diaries*, 189, 186.

38. Nicolson, *Dwight Morrow*, 264–265.

39. Ibid, 307; see especially Ronald Steel, *Walter Lippmann and the American Century* (Boston: Little, Brown and Company, 1980), 235–244.

40. Robert Freeman Smith, "The Morrow Mission and the International Committee of Bankers on Mexico," *Journal of Latin American Studies* 1, no. 2: 152–153.

41. E. W. Kemmerer, "Economic Advisory Work for Governments," *American Economic Review* 17, no. 1 (March 1927): 4.

42. Davis, "Trade Barriers," 73.

3: Building the New Order

1. Thomas Lamont, *Across World Frontiers* (New York: Harcourt, Brace, 1951), 266–267.

2. Arthur M. Johnson, *Winthrop Aldrich* (Boston: Division of Research, Graduate School of Business Administration, Harvard University, 1968), 241.

3. Robert M. Hathaway, "Economic Diplomacy in a Time of Crisis," in *Economics and World Power*, ed. William H. Becker and Samuel F. Wells, Jr. (New York: Columbia University Press, 1984), 281.

4. Stephen V. O. Clarke, *The Reconstruction of the International Monetary System*, Princeton Studies in International Finance, no. 33 (Princeton: International Finance Section, Department of Economics, 1973), 25.

5. Dean Acheson, *Morning and Noon* (Boston: Houghton Mifflin, 1965), 168.

6. *Franklin Delano Roosevelt and Foreign Affairs*, volume 1, ed. Edgar Nixon (Cambridge: Harvard University Press, 1969), 269.

7. Ronald W. Pruessen, *John Foster Dulles: The Road to Power* (New York: Free Press, 1982), 502, 92, 103.

8. Acheson, *Morning and Noon*, 267–275.

9. John Maynard Keynes, "National Self-Sufficiency," *The Yale Review* 22 (Summer 1933): 760.

10. John Morton Blum, *From the Morgenthau Diaries: Years of War* (Boston: Houghton Mifflin, 1967), 474.

11. Keynes, "Self-Sufficiency," 758.

12. Richard N. Gardner, *Sterling-Dollar Diplomacy in Current Perspective* (New York: Columbia University Press, 1980), 49.

13. Alfred E. Eckes, Jr., *A Search for Solvency* (Austin: University of Texas Press, 1975), 39.

14. Gardner, *Sterling-Dollar*, 387, 197.

15. Shepard Morgan, "Constructive Functions of the International Bank," *Foreign Affairs* 9 (July, 1931): 591; see also Robert W. Oliver, *Early Plans for a World Bank*, Princeton Studies in International Finance, no. 29 (Princeton: International Finance Section, Department of Economics, 1971).

16. Cited in Armand Van Dormael, *Bretton Woods* (New York: Holmes and Meier, 1978), 95.

17. Johnson, *Aldrich*, 295–297; and Eckes, *Solvency*, 86, 174–175.

18. R. Gardner, *Sterling-Dollar*, 244.

19. David S. McClellan, *Dean Acheson* (New York: Dodd, Mead, 1976), 94.

20. R. Gardner, *Sterling-Dollar*, 251.

21. Dean Acheson, *Present at the Creation* (New York: Norton, 1969), 727.

22. Lloyd C. Gardner, *Architects of Illusion* (Chicago: Quadrangle, 1970), 219.

23. Arnold A. Rogow, *James Forrestal* (New York: Macmillan, 1963), 336.

24. R. Gardner, *Sterling-Dollar*, 300.

25. McClellan, *Acheson*, 116–117.

26. Preussen, *Dulles*, 309.

27. Richard Mayne, *The Recovery of Europe* (Garden City, N.Y.: Anchor, 1973), 215.

28. Lamont, *Across World Frontiers*, 213.

29. Pruessen, *Dulles*, 92, 103.

30. *Selected Papers of Allan Sproul*, ed. Lawrence Ritter (New York: Federal Reserve Bank of New York, 1980), 83–85.

31. Patric Hendershott and Roger Huang, "Debt and Equity Yields: 1926–80," NBER Working Paper no. 1142 (Cambridge, Mass.: NBER, 1983), 4a.

32. Michael A. Heilperin, "Currency Convertibility—Now," *Fortune*, September 1953, 162.

33. T. A. Wise, "The Bank with the Boardinghouse Reach," *Fortune*, September 1965, 137.

34. Jeremy Main, "Our First Real International Bankers," *Fortune*, December 1967, 144.

35. In U.S. Congress, Joint Economic Committee, Subcommittee on International Exchange and Payments, *International Payments Imbalances and the Need for Strengthening International Financial Arrangements: Hearings* (Washington: Government Printing Office, 1961).

4: The Euromarkets

1. Paul Einzig, "Some Recent Changes in the Euro-Dollar System," *Journal of Finance* 19, no. 3 (September 1964): 444. An excellent source on the contemporary offshore markets is M. S. Mendelsohn, *Money on the Move* (New York: McGraw-Hill, 1980); the staff working papers of the International Monetary Fund are also useful, while the most reliable statistical sources on international banking are publications of the Bank for International Settlements.

2. Eugene Birnbaum, "A Cure for Monetary Discord," *Fortune*, May 1973, 211.

3. Robert Ball, "International Banking Gets the Team Spirit," *Fortune*, June 1972, 100.

4. William F. Butler, "The Future of the Eurodollar Market," *Euromoney*, May 1970, 4.

5. Julien-Pierre Koszul, "Trends in Eurodollars," *Euromoney*, February 1970, 26.

6. Ibid, 27.

7. Henrik Ibsen, *The League of Youth*, 4.

8. Walter Wriston, *Risk and Other Four-Letter Words* (New York: Harper & Row, 1986), jacket.

9. See Joan Spero, *The Failure of the Franklin National Bank* (New York: Columbia University Press, 1980).

5: Lenders and Borrowers

1. As in, for example, the council's 1980 *Annual Report*, pp. 17, 40–41.

2. Debt, borrowing, and current-account figures in this chapter are those of the International Monetary Fund, as presented in IMF staff working papers. Figures for GDP and exports are from *World Tables* (Washington: World Bank, 1976) and various issues of the World Bank's annual *World Development Report*. For more information, see my "Third World Indebted Industrialization," *International Organization* 33, no. 3 (Summer 1981): 407–431, and my "The Brazilian Borrowing Experience," *Latin American Research Review*, 22, no. 1 (1987).

3. *Business Week*, 13 August, 1984, 48.

4. *Euromoney*, Survey, April 1977, 30.

5. *Euromoney*, October 1977, 65.

6. William Kitchenman, "Arms Transfers and Indebtedness of Less Developed Countries," Rand Note no. N-2020-FF (Santa Monica: Rand, 1983).

7. Figures on lending and rescheduling are from Maxwell Watson, et al., *International Capital Markets: Developments and Prospects, 1984* (Washington: IMF, 1984): 64–76, 80.

8. Funaro in *Senhor*, 26 September 1984, 64; Franco in *Jornal do Brasil*, 30 July 1983.

9. Antonio Ermirio de Moraes in *Conjuntura Economica*, August 1982, 65.

10. *Veja*, 9 February 1983, 15.

11. *Senhor*, 26 September 1984.

6: The Future of International Finance

1. Walter Wriston, *Risk and Other Four-Letter Words* (New York: Harper & Row, 1986), 129.

2. Ibid, 133, 141.

3. Ibid, 198.

4. Ibid, 187.

5. Anthony M. Solomon, "Restoring Balance in an Interdependent World," (mimeo, 1982), 2, 9.

6. Wriston, *Risk*, 203.

7. A seminal statement of the problem is Richard N. Cooper, *The Economics of Interdependence* (New York: McGraw-Hill, 1968).

8. Henry Wallich, "Methods of Strengthening Capital Movements to Developing Countries," (mimeo, 1981), 4, 15.

9. Henry Kaufman, "The Challenges Facing American Business," *Euromoney*, September 1975, 104.

10. "Reflation is Fine, but Investment the Real Problem," *Euromoney*, February 1975, 5.

11. "The Real Cost of World Debt," *Wall Street Journal*, 9 February 1983, 30.

12. Federal Reserve Bank of New York, *Quarterly Review*, Autumn 1983, 1–5.

13. *Economist*, 1 October 1983, 66.

14. U.S. Senate, Committee on Foreign Relations, Subcommittee on International Economic Policy, "Global Economic Outlook: Hearings, January 10, January 19, February 1, and April 13, 1983" (Washington, U.S. Government Printing Office, 1983), 502, 504, 505, 506.

15. At the time of the debate, Donald Regan—whose background was in domestic operations for Merrill Lynch—was Treasury secretary; Beryl

Sprinkel, a monetarist economist, was under secretary of the Treasury; and Richard McNamar was deputy secretary of the Treasury.

16. Peter Brimelow, "Why the U.S. Shouldn't Fill the IMF's Till," *Fortune*, 14 November 1983, 58.

17. U.S. House of Representatives, Committee on Banking, Finance, and Urban Affairs, "International Financial Markets and Related Problems: Hearings, February 2, 8, and 9, 1983" (Washington: Government Printing Office, 1983), 1.

7: Invested Interests and American Politics

1. Andrew F. Brimmer, "Eurodollars and the U.S. Balance of Payments," *Euromoney*, December 1969, 13.

2. H. Robert Heller, "The International Challenge—How Will America Respond?" (mimeo, 1987), 11.

3. Robert Heller, "Future Directions in the Financial Services Industry: The International Markets" (mimeo, 1987), 13.

4. *New York Times*, 12 May 1985, E: 5.

5. Gary Hufbauer, et al., *Trade Protection in the United States* (Washington: Institute for International Economics, 1986), 249–262.

6. Garth L. Mangum, Stephen L. Mangum, and Sae Young Kim, "The High Cost of Peace in Steel," *Challenge*, July–August 1986, 47–50.

7. *Wall Street Journal*, 17 December 1985, 10.

8. *Wall Street Journal*, 28 December 1984, 1.

9. Hufbauer, et al., 21, 139–153.

10. *Business Week*, 15 April 1985, 70.

11. Howard D. Samuel, "Coping with the New Realities in Industrial Relations," *Labor Law Journal*, August 1986, 534.

12. *New York Times*, 13 July 1986, section 3, 11.

13. *Labor Law Journal*, August 1986, 454, 540.

14. Samuel, *Coping*, 534.

15. Michael Wallerstein, "The Micro-Foundations of Solidarity: Protectionist Policies, Welfare Policies, and Union Centralization" (mimeo, 1986).

16. Robert Lawrence, *Can America Compete?* (Washington: Brookings Institution, 1984), 78.

17. *New York Times*, 13 July 1986, section 3, 10–11.

18. C. Fred Bergsten, *The World Economy in the 1980s* (Lexington, Mass.: Lexington Books, 1981), 20.

19. Paul Volcker, "Remarks before the 13th American-German Biennial Conference, Dallas, Texas, March 30, 1985," 10–12.

20. *New York Times*, 9 June 1985.

21. See, for example, *Wall Street Journal*, 10 November 1986, 1; *Economist*, 14 September 1985, 59–60.

For further reading

Becker, William H. and Samuel F. Wells, Editors. *Economics and World Power: An Assessment of American Diplomacy Since 1789.* New York: Columbia University Press, 1984.

Bryant, Ralph. *International Financial Intermediation.* Washington: Brookings Institution, 1987.

Cohen, Benjamin J. *In Whose Interest? International Banking and American Foreign Policy.* New Haven: Yale University Press, 1986.

Diaz-Alejandro, Carlos. "Latin American Debt." *Brookings Papers on Economic Activity,* 2 (1984).

Economic Commission for Latin America and the Caribbean. *External Debt in Latin America.* Boulder: Lynne Rienner, 1985.

Gardner, Richard. *Sterling-Dollar Diplomacy in Current Perspective.* New York: Columbia University Press, 1980.

Mendelsohn, M.S. *Money on the Move: The Modern International Capital Market.* New York: McGraw-Hill, 1980.

Munro, Dana G. *Intervention and Dollar Diplomacy in the Caribbean 1900–1920.* Princeton: Princeton University Press, 1964.

Sampson, Anthony. *The Money Lenders: Bankers and a World in Turmoil.* New York: Viking, 1981.

Schuker, Stephen A. *The End of French Predominance in Europe: The Financial Crisis of 1924 and the Adoption of the Dawes Plan.* Chapel Hill: University of North Carolina Press, 1976.

Versluysen, Eugene L. *The Political Economy of International Finance.* London: Gower, 1981

Index